Networks that *Work*

A Practitioner's Guide to Managing Networked Action

SECOND EDITION

Paul Vandeventer
President & CEO, Community Partners

Myrna Mandell, Ph.D.
Co-Author/Network Management Advisor and Researcher

Hershey | Cause, Editing, Production, Promotion

Corky Retson, Design

This book was made possible through the support of The California Endowment.

Library of Congress Number 2001012345
ISBN 978-0-615-32193-6

Contents

Acknowledgements

THIS BOOK – and now this second edition – would not have been possible without the support, contributions and inspiration of the host of network managers, members, funders, practitioners and thinkers working worldwide to solve problems through networked action. Too often these good people find themselves outside the defined boundaries – and attendant comforts – of a professional "field" from which they might draw support and understanding. We hope this book in some small way will help them feel connected to a profoundly skilled and resourceful group of colleagues, to a rich reservoir of scholarly and practical knowledge and to powers and possibilities they may not have recognized they possessed.

Katherine McFate and **Mara Manus**, then program officers at Rockefeller Foundation and Ford Foundation, respectively, opened a very early window for me on the problems and challenges of managing effectively in networked settings. Jointly, they commissioned my organization, Community Partners, to help them advise one of their joint grantees, a network comprised of dozens of member organizations, on how the group might construct its governance and operations. The group adopted 95% of the recommendations we made in our report, and Katherine (then a Ford Foundation program officer and now head of OMB Watch in Washington D.C.) suggested that parts of the report might adapt nicely to "an article, a book or a guide" for funders and network members facing similar complex network management scenarios. I felt I knew too little at that time to take the matter further. Still, Katherine had plucked a responsive chord in me with her faith and keen interest in the value of more widely sharing network management knowledge.

During the following few years, I kept returning to the subject with increasing fascination and urgency. Community Partners was taking on the work of sponsoring and advising the leaders of groups variously describing themselves as coalitions, collaboratives, alliances, partnerships, councils, leagues and sometimes even networks. We needed stronger grounding to serve them well.

Linda Fowells, my colleague and now executive vice president at Community Partners, served first as a valuable sounding board and then as a problem-solving peer in exploring network management intricacies.

David Booher, Senior Policy Advisor for the Center for Collaborative Policy at California State University, Sacramento, provided very early inspiration with his explanations of the ubiquity of conflict in networks and the need for robust conflict management and facilitation as an integral part of any network effort.

Dutch researcher **Dr. Erik-Hans Klijn**, editor with Walter J. M. Kickert and Joop F. M. Koppenjan of the priceless book *Managing Complex Networks: Strategies for the*

Public Sector, responded to an email I sent him in 2005. My email appreciated the masterful academic rendering of network management challenges and solutions collected by Dr. Klijn and his colleagues. I proposed writing a more practical guide targeted at field-level network practitioners and useful to funders investing grant funds in supporting networks. Dr. Klijn wrote a very encouraging note in reply and connected me with a valued colleague and collaborator.

From the far reaches of the Netherlands, Dr. Klijn directed me to my very own Southern California backyard. There I found **Myrna Mandell**, a perceptive and spirited adventurer and researcher at California State University, Northridge near Los Angeles. Myrna agreed to conduct three case study interviews, inform the early outlines for the book, respond to drafts of fleshed-out narratives and generally bind herself to this project as an intellectual partner.

Dr. Robert Ross, **The California Endowment** – along with then program officers **Paul Hernandez** and **Amanda Rounsaville** – provided encouragement, infectious excitement and board-approved grant funding that allowed time to develop the book.

Living with *Networks that Work* since its first printing in 2007 has placed its utility to others in considerable perspective. In workshops, consultations and classrooms, not to mention from many practitioners privately, we receive appreciation for a book many tell us they wish had been at their fingertips "when we began this work."

With this second edition, we have:

- Made editing changes throughout the book.
- Added cooperating and coordinating case material.
- Inserted (with the permission of Sage Publications) an illuminating chart comparing management in network settings vs. classic organizational settings from Kickert, Klijn and Koopenjan's *Managing Complex Networks*.
- Added two useful summary charts titled "When to Form a Network," courtesy of Professor Robert Agranoff of Indiana University, and "Why Not to Form a Network," expertly summarized by Bob (with our appreciation!) from our work in this book.

When I show the chart from *Managing Complex Networks* to network practitioners, I watch light bulbs brighten in their brains. I enjoy seeing how the chart helps them have the same "Aha!" I experienced upon first seeing the chart.

Many more thanks to the people who thoughtfully reviewed the content, provided their thoughts or added bits of expertise and wisdom: **David Chatfield**, **Jeanna Keller Berdel**, **Alison De Lucca**, **Anna Diaz** (a wonderful and thoughtful editor!), **Anne Duncan**, **Cynthia Freeman**, **Judy Harper**, **Anna Henderson**, **Eve Hill**, **Chuck Hirt**, **Laura Hogan**, **Anna Karailieva**, **Dylan Kendall**, **Lyndee Knox**, **Igor Kokarev**, **Mara Manus**, **Katherine McFate**, **Eric Medina**, **Laura O'Loughlin**, **Ellen Sanchez**, **Yolanda Vera**, **Gwen Walden**, **Belinda Walker**, **Billie Weiss** and **Eugene Wilson**.

Special thanks to **Corky Retson**, our gifted designer, and the production team that guided the first printing at **Hershey | Cause**: editor **Kirsty Burkhart**, proofreader **Patty Park**, and the firm's irrepressible principal, **R. Christine Hershey**.

Our immense gratitude goes to the network members who shared their experiences for the case studies:

Southern California College Access Network: Alison De Lucca

NAAFE: Joe Berry, Jeremy Brecher, Tim Costello, Marcus Courtney, Kim Foltz, Suren Moodliar, Cathy Ruckleshaus

Child Care Alliance of Los Angeles: Grace Cainoy Weltman

The California Partnership: Nancy Berlin, Mary Ignatius, Alicia Lepe, Joseph Villela

The Water Forum: Jeff Loux, Jonas Minton, Walt Pettit, Susan Sherry, Leo Winternitz

Paul Vandeventer
November 2011

Why *Networks that Work* Now?

JUST AS INVESTORS like Bill Gates and Warren Buffett pool philanthropic resources to tackle global issues on an enormous scale, groups across social, governmental and commercial sectors realize the need for similar collective "networked" action. Nonprofit organizations seek to amplify their missions by finding and negotiating common ground from which to work in stride with other social sector groups. Businesses form strategic alliances. Governments fashion joint powers agreements. Powerful cross-sector alliances form that change entire public systems (witness the coming reforms in the American health care system). At the core of all this inter-organizational work, success lies in effective network management.

In the simplest terms, a "network" refers to any sustained effort around which different, autonomous organizations work in concert as equal partners in pursuit of a common social, civic, public interest or even commercial purpose. In the best instances, groups move from independence to new kinds of interdependence.

Perhaps because our world has become increasingly complex, organizations, agencies and institutions are now more likely than ever before to form networks to tackle environmental, health care, childhood, aging and any number of other crises. Their leaders recognize the need to leverage trusted relationships with other leaders, extending in the process limited organizational resources and strengthening on-the-ground results.

Leaders recognize the need to leverage trusted relationships with other [organizations].

Unfortunately, coming together doesn't always mean working well together. Some networks frankly don't work. Bowing to a funder's grant application requirement and slapping together a "collaborative" that has no relationship substance forms a shaky basis at best for future network success. Ignoring histories and the leftover residue of old conflicts can torpedo chances of finding common ground and shared purpose. Failed networks can squander resources, including trust, time and momentum.

Honest self-assessment, careful planning, clear understandings, skilled facilitative leadership and early identification of areas where conflict likely will arise can help avoid and overcome obstacles. The case studies abbreviated in the appendix and fully fleshed out at www.CommunityPartners.org/networks provide useful examples of how a few groups created networks that really work and the success they can achieve.

The Genesis of *Networks That Work*

This book resulted from years of observation and experience. As do many helpful tools, this one emerged from frustration and perplexity. At Community Partners, where scores of civic initiatives incubate and receive fiscal sponsorship under our umbrella, we repeatedly saw alliances and coalitions of nonprofit groups form, struggle and, too often, fail.

Digging deeper for causes, we realized many groups undertaking these ventures defaulted to classical organizational planning and management approaches. They applied strategic planning complexity where network planning simplicity would have served them better by freeing their energies for joint work. Large groups of autonomous organizations with different histories, divergent views of the same societal problem, strong-willed leaders, and commitments to carefully hewn missions needed better tools to finish work they set out to accomplish together. Networks, we discovered, seemed to do better when tended by the deft and gentle hand of a facilitative leader rather than the executive hand of a director.

Successful network members defined the purpose of working together, established their most urgent priorities and got right to the critical tasks and activities that would help them achieve their purpose. They negotiated trade-offs and working relationships – how to govern their union – as the work unfolded and its complexity became clear. In the best situations, joint work undertaken in a network setting would eventually feed results back into the organizational strategic planning of individual network member groups. Often, network members found that productive work in the network setting resulted in alignment between what they were doing in the network and what went on with both programs and planning back in their own organizations. Conflict, we realized, was never far from the surface in most networks, but where network members anticipated and planned ways to manage it, they were able to effectively work through the difficulties of moving from self-interest to common purpose.

We saw the degree to which attention to building relationships among network members mattered fundamentally to network success. Networks where key members had pre-existing relationships, even if those relationships were conflicted, needed less time to get up and running because members knew and understood others with whom they were dealing. And we realized that the genuine interdependence that marks a collaborative network rarely resulted without members risking loss of turf, shifts in the locus of power, changed prestige, re-allocation of money or relinquishment of a long-prized place in a system that needed changing.

We saw a growing need to share these lessons with anyone in the middle of navigating a network venture or about to embark on one.

How to Use This Book

If your organization has joined or is considering a networked effort with other groups, if the scale of your mission seems too daunting or too important to tackle alone, if you're looking to leverage your resources and amplify your organizational power, this book is for you. It covers a range of issues to consider before you decide to engage in a network, as you create a network and while you pursue networked action – all designed to help your network work.

Just as every set of social relationships differ, every network has its own culture and peculiarities. No common template exists, but certain principles do apply. This book is not, nor could it be, a complete guide to network settings in which you'll find yourself involved. Still, it does provide tools useful in evaluating your options and solving certain common network problems. The case examples bring certain challenges and options to life. Checklists and essential questions inform and help organize choices. Samples of helpful materials have been included along with a bibliography for deepening your network knowledge.

We hope this book will serve as an indispensable resource, an orientation to organizational arrangements that expands the breadth and depth of social, civic and institutional effectiveness.

Please share your thoughts with us about this book's utility. Your feedback will help ensure that future editions reflect the experience of network practitioners, respond to needs from the field and increase the value of available literature on network best practices.

Please forward comments, questions and thoughts to networks@CommunityPartners.org.

Chapter 1

What Are Networks?

The term "network" as used in this book refers to many different organizations working in concert as equal partners pursuing a common social or civic purpose over a sustained period of time.

Organizations of all kinds commonly act alone to fulfill civic, community or public interest missions. Sometimes they discover compelling reasons to join forces, even across different sectors – social, commercial, governmental – of the wider civic landscape. Groups that organize themselves in networks do so to achieve greater social, economic or political impact. Sooner or later, even in the fragmented, resource-competitive realm of the American nonprofit sector, everyone recognizes that achieving most organizational missions requires cross-organizational effort. These joint efforts have many different purposes and operate throughout society.

Members in some networks, such as in membership associations that gather individuals from groups operating in the same field, may simply have the purpose of improving information sharing among practitioners and spreading best practices. Other networks build power

A Working Definition

WHAT: **Many different organizations working in concert**
WHO: **Organizations, institutions, governmental agencies, corporations, foundations, etc.**
WHY: **To pursue a common, defined purpose**
HOW: **As equal partners**

and impact through their collective size and strength, coordinating service delivery or joining forces to advance legislative and public policy changes. Some networks come together determined to fundamentally alter entrenched, unwieldy, outmoded or unworkable public systems *from the outside,* using mass organizational mobilization, legislative lobbying and political advocacy. Others, comprised of decision making representatives from all the key system players, gather, often when a system is stressed to the crisis point, to negotiate the trade-offs necessary for change to occur *from the inside.* Networks can bring greater scale and focus, more productive kinds of working relationships and more lasting effectiveness to addressing public problems.

Networks can bring greater scale and focus, more productive kinds of working relationships and more lasting effectiveness to addressing public problems.

Referred to by many different names – like coalition, collaborative, alliance, partnership or league – networks form when knowledgeable people concede that the scale and complexity of a societal problem exceeds any single organization's capacity to tackle it alone. Savvy, practical leaders recognize that many organizations working jointly to address a large problem may also make their independent work easier to accomplish.

Distinctive Features of Networks

Three critical features distinguish networks from the individual organizations and institutions that comprise them:

1. Network settings require members to invest in and build new types of relationships and, in varying ways and degrees, acknowledge their mutual interdependence.

2. Networks differ in their level of complexity and, therefore, in the risks they demand of members.
3. No one is "in charge" in a network.

Networks Require New Relationships

The desire to address urgent public problems and important tasks brings network members together. Achieving durable results from working jointly, however, often hinges on how well members relate to one another. Network settings require respectful, open working relationships, and therefore network members must:

- Recognize, prepare to reveal and sometimes negotiate their own organizational and institutional interests.
- Appreciate and respect the interests of other groups, even if that means revising or changing long-held views.
- Mutually acknowledge that starting points for social change – even if network members don't describe or approach the societal problem they want to tackle in exactly the same way – lie in those places where they can find common ground and start working together.

Increasing Complexity Means Different Levels of Risk

Existing research identifies at least three progressively more complex types of networks, each with higher "stakes" or risks for members. Knowing at the outset what risks you can tolerate will help you decide what kind of network you want to form. Organizing one kind of network may lead to a greater tolerance for risk among the groups and the ability to reorganize in new ways with higher stakes.

No One's "In Charge" In A Network

Relationships in networks rest on a principle of equal partnership, which requires special structural and managerial arrangements. Member groups in networks will differ in size, reach, visibility, celebrity, economic power, political strength, reputation, preferred approaches, language and a host of other ways. Negotiating what constitutes the terms of equal partnership becomes an essential early step to keeping common ground in sight and differences in perspective.

Think about it. Executives and managers of independent groups exercise whatever authority they deem necessary to get things done. In their organizational settings, they are in charge. They set direction and goals, decide which opportunities to pursue to meet the mission, make decisions, direct employees and allocate resources. No executive wants to place decisions about what their organization does in any outsider's hands. Working in a network setting, however, requires them to operate from a different perspective.

Networks function on the principle of what researchers label "divided" or "shared" authority. No member can tell another member what to do because all members come from and represent the interests of autonomous and independent organizations. Decisions about network direction require members to negotiate, agree on priorities, honor commitments and account to one another for results. Leveling the field of play and defining terms of equal partnership from the outset help network members prepare to manage inevitable disagreements that come up among leaders accustomed to getting things done their way.

When the work of a network requires staffing the network with a manager or a coordinator (and perhaps other staff as well), all of the network members need to agree on the manager's role and make expectations clear about how they expect the role to be performed. In relation to members of the network, a network manager needs to assert facilitative leadership rather than the kind of directive leadership that works in organizational settings. Certainly a network manager leading a staff needs to give workers direction. But the network members need to agree on priority tasks and activities they want the network to accomplish, and deploy the network manager's time in ways that get results. In highly effective network settings, member organizations may absorb certain managerial or staffing costs of the network. They might agree, for example, to lend certain organizational capabilities (such as research, media communication, regulatory knowledge, technology or financial administration) as part of their commitment to the network's success.

Whether paid employees perform the role of network manager or a group of network members function voluntarily as a management committee or steering group, successful network managers act as process coordinators and facilitators. In general, a network manager:

- Helps members communicate, share information, clarify interests and define genuine differences.
- Helps members identify what tasks need to be performed to fulfill the network's purpose.
- Guides, smoothes and creates efficient interactions as members go about the network's tasks.
- Spots favorable opportunities members can pursue to address and resolve issues that brought the network into existence in the first place.
- Locates and helps secure resources.
- Builds the network by identifying and helping to bring in new members.
- Seeks ways to refresh and renew the network's capabilities and functions.

Relationships in networks rest on a principle of equal partnership, which requires special structural and managerial arrangements.

In short, network managers handle the complexity that naturally arises when large, diverse collections of people work on any project. They do so constantly mindful that they are in service to the greater good embodied in the network's purpose and in the agreements network members have made in deciding to work together.

Three Different Types of Networks

There's a helpful typology in the popular literature that breaks down the different types of networks into three broad categories (see pages 26-27 for examples of each):

Cooperating Networks
Coordinating Networks
Collaborating Networks

Cooperating Networks seem to comprise the greatest number of network arrangements. Member entry and exit occurs with relative ease and individual members don't need to place too much of their organizational autonomy at risk. Members of these types of networks often:

- Find high levels of urgency in gathering to convene problem solving or issue discussion sessions that elevate mutual awareness.
- Use the setting to build a field or gather momentum for the early stages of movements.
- Reach agreement by commonly understood forms of dialogue, negotiation and consensus.
- Model and explain best practices for one another.
- Share information and work jointly to document and gain perspective on problems.
- Test ideas and learn about different approaches to one another's work.
- Create social environments that lead to better personal and professional relationships.
- Experiment with more trust-based forms of engagement.

Coordinating Networks involve low to moderate risk to members. In addition to many of the activities that distinguish cooperating networks, members of coordinating networks often:

- Identify and pursue intentional – even contractually binding – service delivery, joint funding or policy advocacy priorities.
- Negotiate time, resource and energy commitments with other network members.

- Push established organizational boundaries and create a more robust sense of mutual interdependence.
- Strengthen individual and institutional relationships by engaging in activities that require greater mutual reliance.

Collaborating Networks involve high stakes and, therefore, involve higher degrees of member risk. In addition to many of the activities associated with cooperating and coordinating networks, members of collaborating networks often:

- Join together to pursue fundamental, long-term system creation or reform of some kind.
- Constitute their membership from all the necessary players needed to bring about system change.
- Require that representatives at the table come with the authority to speak on behalf of and bind their organizations to network decisions.
- Begin replacing prior notions about how the system worked with new ways it can work differently.
- Agree upon, work within and self-enforce the tasks required to achieve and maintain the new or reformed system.
- Use more robust, even customized methods for anticipating, surfacing, addressing and resolving conflicts.
- Authentically participate in or advocate for fundamental resource reallocation in ways that, under the old system, they may have resisted or protected.
- Reach agreement on how to permanently and often radically shift the ways they once operated.
- Redefine the ways in which they play their various roles within a larger system.

Across the network spectrum, success depends on members participating with their eyes wide open and without delusions or posturing about what they hope to accomplish by working together.

Potential risks for members of a network increase in correlation to the scale of the desired change. At the outset, groups affiliating as networks need to gauge their own comfort with and commitment to change. They need to assess the degree to which the organizations they represent want to invest in fostering change that – in the name of improved public value – may alter policies, systems and resource streams upon which they have grown reliant.

For many groups the risks, constraints, exposure and demands of network participation may be uncomfortable, even unbearable. In such cases, groups always have the choice of operating independently. However, if the leadership of an organization or institution chooses to organize a new network or affiliate with one that already exists, they can create or try to find a setting where the network conditions come with the degree of risk that accords with their comfort.

Types of Networks Illustrated

The major network types cited in this book are **cooperating, coordinating** and **collaborating** networks. The case summaries in the Appendices cover the three different and distinctive network types.

Cooperating Networks

Success depends on members participating with their eyes wide open.

Southern California College Access Network (SoCalCAN) represents a cooperating network - the most common form of network - comprised of organizations homogenous in terms of their laser focus on college access and success for low-income students. Yet the member organizations vary a great deal in terms of history, approach, leadership style, risk tolerance, geographic focus and other features, all of which makes for genuine complexity in finding common ground when working together. [Appendix A]

The North American Alliance for Fair Employment (NAAFE) illustrates another cooperating network. Member groups varied widely from direct service, to organizing, to policy advocacy and legal work. Through small working groups, members pursued a variety of activities intended to result in larger system reforms. As a result, a number of campaigns were highly successfu in disseminating information on a variety of issues. The group as a whole valued a high degree of sharing among autonomous and independent organizations and the risks they took tended to cross very little into the organizational boundaries each group considered its own. [Appendix B]

Coordinating Networks

The Child Care Alliance of Los Angeles (CCALA) and The California Partnership both illustrate the behavior of coordinating networks. Members work together to carefully synchronize key activities while each organization maintains autonomy. CCALA members spell out their network common ground in the form of aligned public contracts with governmental agencies funding childcare services. The California Partnership members align policy advocacy activities, bringing the power of many organizational voices and constituencies into focus in state and local legislative bodies.

Coordinating networks come together on issues that affect most or all of the member organizations; members work toward specific agreements on tasks and activities that will benefit them individually and collectively. They take more risks, but still maintain their independent status as separate organizations. Working toward high levels of agreement, members may execute formal contracts to which all are party (as in the case of CCALA) or advance a unified front on public policy (as with The California Partnership). [Appendices C and D]

Collaborating Networks

The Water Forum illustrates the behavior and character of a collaborating network. The organizations in this network, after decades of litigation and conflict, have come together to work on complex issues of water resource allocation, regulation and watershed or habitat protection that none could successfully resolve alone. The members spent a lot of time recognizing their essential interdependence and the need to change the ways they conducted business. They concentrated on building new relationships and establishing trust among members who previously only had contentious relationships. Willing to look at their fundamental approach to water issues, the network members made major changes across a complex system of water delivery and watershed management. They have agreed to work together for 30 years and recognize the need to take great risks. [Appendix E]

CHAPTER 2

What to Consider *Before* You Start

With All the Risk and Hard Work, Why Form a Network?

WORKING IN NETWORKS can prove challenging, even difficult. As noted earlier, not every group has the appetite for the risk, potential conflict, commitment of time and resources or hard work. Too often, groups allow funders and others to push them into working together when they are poorly prepared for the endeavor and have no prior relationship base upon which to build. Terms like collaboratives, alliances, leagues, partnerships and coalitions get thrown around routinely as if success is just a matter of gathering well-intentioned folks around the same table. Working from the wrong motivations or without appreciation for the negotiation of interests necessary for any multi-organizational network to succeed can thwart progress in addressing large societal problems. It can leave critical players out of the process, waste resources, disappoint expectations and even hurt people in vulnerable communities.

But the right motivations can unleash creative energy, advancing needed change and leading to fundamentally reformed organizational relationships, public policies and social systems. As critical as they are, these motivations often only rise to the surface as organizations jointly examine shared interests. This examination – best conducted first in the private counsel of each organization and then among prospective network members in joint counsel with one another – helps everyone understand and come to grips with their fundamental tolerance for risk. Only by knowing, revealing and negotiating interests can groups decide where on the continuum of risk tolerance they stand. Groups unwilling to open themselves up to certain levels of risk do not belong in network relationships. Only by knowing where they stand can groups decide if the risks of working in a network setting outweigh the safety of operating independently.

The right motivations can unleash creative energy, advancing needed change and leading to fundamentally reformed organizational relationships, public policies and social systems.

Many routes exist to weighing the advantages and disadvantages of networked action before venturing further ahead.

Risks, Pitfalls, Problems and Solutions

In building a network, organizations may need to tackle a number of challenges head on, particularly any outfalls or unresolved issues arising from past experiences. If left unaddressed, organizational histories, distinctive preferences for ways of working and attitudes about working jointly with other groups can prevent consensus building; these issues tend to hinder effectiveness and lead to misunderstandings or flawed assumptions. Committed social sector players can handle these challenges. However, sometimes they may want to enlist the services of skilled facilitators equipped with problem-solving and interest-negotiation tools. These resource people can accelerate the network toward effective action by training network members in everything from meeting management to high-level conflict resolution.

Issues likely to need surfacing, working through and, sometimes, early stage defusing include:

- Members tied to unique organizational histories, ideologies or peculiarities: a situation that can become as exasperating as it is counterproductive to working with others.
- Member insistence that everyone see "the problem we're trying to address" in exactly the same way: a formula for endless argument and needless conformity.
- Strong or exclusive member claims to particular physical, programmatic, political, operational, demographic and even moral territory or "turf."
- A misinformed view that network planning and classic organizational strategic planning are one and the same.
- Insistence upon particular approaches to and methods for solving problems: a scenario likely to impair creative thinking and hinder effective action.
- Impatience with "process" among network members habituated or predisposed to action: a leaning that fails to recognize the extent to which – in network settings just as inside any classic organization – helping people understand and evaluate what they are doing generally produces a better result than if people act blindly or with partial knowledge.

If the previous points are not addressed at the very beginning or if network members fail to create space for addressing them as they emerge, a number of other challenges or problems will arise, including:

- Lost investments of time, energy and resources if different groups fail to see that agreement to a clearly defined joint purpose respects everyone's particular take on "the problem" and frees the network to turn its attention to important priorities, tasks and activities.

- Potentially lethal land mines if groups refuse up front to face conflict-producing issues and whatever relational, competitive or historic tensions that may divide them.
- Misunderstandings and potential offense if members fail to treat one another as equal partners – even when the social, political or economic strength of individual groups differs.
- Undue complication of otherwise ordinary issues (communications, financial administration, management standards and ways of working through conflict) that arise any time many groups work together.
- Deflated expectations – and possible reluctance to work together in the future – if groups aspire to an ambitious purpose and then neglect to dedicate human, financial and other resources to its fulfillment.
- Individual feelings of disempowerment, betrayal, burnout, fatigue and hopelessness resulting from poor management.

Still, these hurdles can be overcome in a variety of ways if network members consciously:

- Understand from the outset that the momentum of working in a network setting to achieve any agreed-upon purpose improves when members can recognize and celebrate incremental "wins" in the short term as the network develops.

- Strive to reframe problems or issues in ways that step back from members' individual perspectives and seek a new perspective rooted in the key areas of agreement among all members.
- Recognize from the beginning that network settings differ from classic organizational settings and require new modes of planning, new ways of working and even new ways of talking. Members may need to develop new skills in areas such as meeting management, problem solving and conflict resolution. Training and counsel may help them acquire these skills more quickly than just toughing it out and learning from hard experience.
- Come to the network setting with the knowledge and sanction of their home organizations, something that will give them the authority to make decisions critical to advancing the network.
- Insist all representatives at the network table routinely advise leaders in their home organizations of the progress, difficulties and commitments the organization has made – and must honor – to the other members of the network.
- Make certain the key decision makers, not the day-to-day representatives, from the parent organizations commit their organizations by signing any network agreements.

Even as they acknowledge the potential challenges that may arise, groups considering working in these settings want to also keep the advantages in clear focus.

Some Advantages of Networks

Despite – and sometimes as a direct result of – the challenges of forming, networks can and do work on multiple levels. They can help focus both independent and collective efforts, expand best practices and amplify results. Indeed, organizations working together in networks can realize a variety of distinct advantages, including:

- More effectively delivered services that meaningfully address human needs, improve civic life and enable people to determine their own destiny and that of their community.
- Greater influence and power through larger numbers and sharper focus.
- Greater impact through aligned activities.
- Durable agreements that form the basis for sustained commitment to genuine interdependence and lead to wider, more lasting changes.
- Strengthened, more trusting personal and professional relationships achieved through openness and shared struggle toward solving public problems.
- Greater knowledge of others' approaches and methods.

Given both the potential risks and advantages, no group should enter lightly into creating or participating in a network. Thoughtful assessment is critical when evaluating network participation and tolerances for risk.

Checklist: Four Key Questions

When weighing the pros and cons of forming a network, asking four key questions can help. They include:

1. Do we really want to do this?
2. What do we hope to accomplish?
3. Who do we need to have with us?
4. How will we fund the both the network's management and its activities?

The checklists beneath each question will help leaders assess whether network participation is right for their organizations.

1. Do we really want to do this?

Forming networks involves new risks and inevitable difficulties: long-range time and resource commitment, vulnerability to outside scrutiny, potential accountability to others, tolerance for operational differences and the possibility of lasting change.

- Can we commit sufficient time and resources? Networks require long-term member investments of money, staff time, material and intellectual energy, always with the expectation that such jointly committed resources will reciprocally advance each group's independent mission. The return on such investments will likely accumulate over time rather than appear immediately. Network members need to temper expectations, commit to a shared purpose and strive for flexibility in response to shifting priorities and emerging opportunities. Results will emerge from a focus on achievable near-term tasks and activities selected for their contribution to cumulative long-term benefits.

- Are we ready for intense scrutiny? Sustained time across the table from other groups invariably opens up any organization's values, interests and effectiveness to critical examination. To prepare, conduct a searching internal self-assessment, check the resilience of your organizational ego, know your interests and risk tolerance and get your internal house in order.

- Are we prepared to hold ourselves accountable to agreements? Effective networks require that members achieve clarity – while maintaining a certain level of flexibility – about the purpose that brings them together. Out of that will emerge agreement about priority action areas and the kinds of tasks and activities members will need to engage in both through their own organizations and through the network. Agreements carry with them the implicit expectation that members will seriously strive to achieve results.

- Can we tolerate differences with the way other groups work? Unique organizational cultures and histories mean that no two organizations will ever likely share the same exact definition of the societal problem they want to solve or the goals they will pursue in solving it. One network advantage is that groups can maintain their autonomy and march to their own beat, even as the network setting helps them align their efforts with other groups. Yet networks can falter if they lack methods for dealing with members that block progress, whose representatives don't participate or whose behavior proves disruptive or destructive. For best results, approach network participation expecting wide variation in perspectives and differences in problem solving approaches.

- HOW PREPARED ARE WE TO PURSUE AUTHENTIC CHANGE? Forming or joining a network can lead to or stem from the recognition that the *status quo* no longer works – in a service delivery system, in a set of public policies or among agency leaders who do not know one another or work together. To varying degrees, networks demand or result in real and lasting change in systems, institutional relationships, policies, programs and funding streams. Enter network settings assuming that change will occur and understand your willingness to experience the consequences.

2. What do we hope to accomplish?

Define the core purpose that binds network members together. Even if it evolves over time, the motivating purpose, captured in writing, represents the clearest statement about what the network wants to accomplish. Clarity of purpose also helps shape understanding of the type of network (cooperating, coordinating or collaborating), requires members to examine their organizational self-interest in relation to others, and allows them to create a structure that embraces both the opportunity and the associated risks.

- DO WE EMBRACE AND HAVE WE PARTICIPATED IN SHAPING THE NETWORK'S PURPOSE? To streamline information sharing and build better relationships among groups, forming a cooperating network with relatively low levels of risk and resource demand may prove optimal. Shared activities may include a website or social media forum with chat or blog capabilities, regular print or online newsletters, sharing of in-depth case studies, news reports and scholarly research, and periodic gatherings combining learning and social interaction. For achieving larger-scale change, defining the common purpose may require more time, introspection on core organizational self-interests, and finding ways to surface and resolve inevitable differences with other groups. Given the higher risks and greater resource commitments of coordinating and collaborating networks, consider and adopt reliable governance structures and robust methods for resolving the problems and disputes likely to arise in the course of the network's life.

One network advantage is that groups can maintain their autonomy and march to their own beat, even as the network setting helps them align their efforts with other groups.

- Can the network's purpose advance our organizational or institutional mission? If it doesn't, what's the point of becoming part of the network in the first place? Organizational self-interest must be a component of network participation – though not the exclusive or even primary driver. The broader network purpose, along with the network's priorities, tasks and activities, should energize the work inside member organizations. Commitment to participate in a network should be a complete organizational commitment, an extension of the goals and programs of the organization, not an afterthought or sideline activity. A section of any organizational strategic plan needs to include and account for network commitments so organizational resources have legitimacy. If becoming part of a network feels like an organizational burden, something clearly is amiss and requires deeper exploration. That said, network members must expect to seriously negotiate interests, trade-offs and risks in service to the common purpose – the shared interests – that bind the network together.

- ARE STRONG MECHANISMS IN PLACE TO WORK STEADILY TOWARD ACHIEVING THE NETWORK PURPOSE? Clear articulation of purpose and the development of working relationships and processes can be frustrating. Even when personal and organizational relationships have strong, deep roots, some communal "storming" must occur before the group figures out the best path forward with the fewest obstacles. Groups need clarity about themselves and the history of the problem they are uniting to address as they make choices about what activities and structures will support their efforts. Some may need outside consultants with sufficient skills, competency and objectivity to facilitate working relationships among network members. Skilled facilitators or even mediators can help the group get over tough spots and train network members in conflict-resolution and interest-negotiation techniques. Networks may also require staff with a variety of network management, planning, negotiation, communications, technology, resource development, financial and administrative skills.

3. Who do we need to have with us?

When evaluating a potential network, take into account the players needed at the table and who must have investment in the network's purpose, as well as those who need to support the network in other ways.

- What's the right size and composition of the network's membership? The selection and number of network members should bear a strong correlation to the purpose the network seeks to fulfill. Depending on the purpose, the network may require participation by members from different sectors – commercial, civic, nonprofit, governmental or labor.

- Do all members need to share the same point of view? Take into account participation by groups with different or even conflicting definitions of what's wrong that needs fixing. They may be essential to enlist. Consciously and carefully approach any decisions to ignore or exclude organized interest groups operating outside – and potentially at cross-purposes with – the network. These decisions are important because the ignored or excluded will very likely affect priorities as the network progresses.

- Does every group need to have the same level of commitment to the network? Some networks may define varying levels of participation for different organizations or groups. For example, individuals not affiliated with or directly representing organizations may still bring value to the network and be welcomed with modified resource commitment expectations. Some networks grant "observer" or "expert resource" status to representatives who are not direct network members, but who can learn from or bring value to the network's deliberative process. Even while thinking about participants, consider the range of outside support the network will need to succeed. Subject matter experts or academics may provide critical information, perspective and analysis.

- Does our network need other kinds of supporters? Equally important, and perhaps supremely so, make sure that influential people – think "movers and shakers" – in the community or within the arena of the network's purpose support the network. These "sponsors" can provide critical civic sanction to network activities, protecting the network activities while embracing its purpose. Sponsors may include past or present legislators or other public officials, respected leaders of funding organizations, past or present university presidents, legal system luminaries and other people of indisputable civic stature. Although not necessarily members of the network, sponsors lend their prestige and blessing to the network and ensure its legitimacy, elevate its activities and accomplishments and confer tacit approval – even insulation from assaults on credibility – that can make a difference to continued network operation.

4. How will we fund both the network's management and its activities?

Network operational expenses can vary greatly depending on what members intend to accomplish and their expectations of network activities.

- How expensive is participating in the network going to be? To the degree that some level of expense will accompany the network's operation, expect to participate in footing the costs or securing outside resources. Simply stated, funding and resource commitment demands come with the territory. The more challenging the landscape, the greater the need will be for funds to sustain the network. That said, money and other resources should ease, not impede, network effectiveness. Networks have found surprisingly creative ways to meet the necessary resource commitments, some of which will receive greater attention later on in this book.

- WHAT ASSETS SHOULD WE PREPARE TO BRING TO THE TABLE? Recognize from the outset that any network's greatest assets lie in the mission focus, leadership strength, program vigor, fiscal and administrative stability, and funding relationships that already exist within member organizations. The old adage that "a chain is as strong as its weakest link" applies here. Strong, stable and reasonably well-funded network member organizations can enhance and even accelerate a network's effectiveness. Financially weak and otherwise anemic members should not assume they will somehow reap financial windfalls from network participation. In anticipating network resource demands, determine what network functions require cash and which can be supplied in-kind by member organizations. If the network collectively decides to approach funders to support core network operations, funders may want to know the actual cash value of collective member resources committed to the network's success. That members might actually think about and document such value well before being asked speaks volumes about the importance they place on participating in the network.

The selection and number of network members should bear a strong correlation to the purpose the network seeks to fulfill.

- SHOULD WE EXPECT TO GAIN FINANCIALLY BY PARTICIPATING IN A NETWORK? Groups need to have the fiscal vision and confidence, coupled with the steadiness of commitment, to see that network success will likely feed long-term organizational success in addressing critical social, system and policy problems. Achieving large gains in those arenas generally makes for a good investment of organizational assets. Still, as many times as networks form simply in response to funder's dangling resources asking for collaborative grant proposals, the hope of gaining immediate fiscal advantage is the least constructive reason for joining a network. More than one network has formed around the availability of money and fallen apart as soon as that money stream dried up.

- WHAT OTHER CONSIDERATIONS ABOUT MONEY SHOULD WE THINK ABOUT IN ADVANCE? Consider and appreciate that there are certain stability advantages that come with sustained and reliable funding streams. There are also trade-offs depending on the source of funds. Foundation and other outside, non-network members may want to impose expectations or controls. The relationship between who funds the network and any expectations of control attached to funding need to be thought through carefully.

After weighing all the considerations, if you decide to organize a network, you will need to address many specific topics and logistics. The next chapter poses 14 essential questions designed to help prospective network members move toward creating a new or participating in an existing network.

Chapter 3

What to Consider As You Create A Network

Fourteen Essential Questions

The questions discussed on the following pages have an obvious logic to their sequence. No doubt you will invariably find yourself considering aspects of all the questions simultaneously as formative deliberations proceed. Keep a record of issues raised and decisions made around each question during this process to facilitate the drafting of a network agreement (sometimes called a memorandum of understanding, a network charter or a relational contract; see *Sample Template for a Network Agreement* provided as Appendix E) when the time comes to do so. Essential questions to address include:

- What urgent purpose drives our network?
- What determines network participation and defines who should join the network?
- How firm is member commitment to this network?
- To what extent does the network have continuous outside support or sponsorship?
- How do we determine and organize our action priorities?
- How will we organize, manage and govern the network?

- What methods will we use to establish new relationships?
- How will we conduct our work?
- What kind of agreement should we make to function as a network?
- How do network members hold themselves and one another accountable?
- How will we resolve conflicts?
- What funding and other resources will the network need, and where will the support come from?
- What are the challenges of funder-driven networks?
- What other key resources do we need to have in place?

1. What urgent purpose drives our network?

Shared purpose among member organizations drives all networks. Take care not to confuse purpose and problem. Defining the network's shared purpose differs from reaching universal agreement on the social, civic or public interest problem as each member organization may define it. Because every member organization brings a different history, perspective and organizational mission to the network, any hope of achieving universal agreement on the problem may remain elusive. Instead, focus on crafting a clear, specific and unambiguous statement of the network's purpose.

For example, The Water Forum, one of the groups profiled on pages 26-27, expressed its two-pronged purpose as follows:

- Provide a reliable and safe water supply for the Sacramento region's economic health and planned

development to the year 2030; and,
- Preserve the fishery, wildlife, recreational and aesthetic values of the Lower American River.

There's little ambiguity – though a great deal of in-built tension – to such a purpose even taking into account the four distinctive groups of network members: water agencies, a municipal and a county government, developers and environmental organizations. Its duality reveals precisely what the network's 40 or so member organizations will need to grapple with continuously throughout their planned decades of affiliation. This is a network whose members have agreed to operate in a system dedicated to finding balance between development and economic interests on one hand and environmental and aesthetic concerns on the other. It is no easy feat to achieve this purpose; in fact, achieving it may be the wrong conceptual framework through which to view the Water Forum. Rather, the network functions as a bounded place where committed partners recognize and remain aware of the changing physical, political, economic and social natures of their region. Voluntarily self-governing, the forum acts as a locus for mutual accountability, a check on unrestrained behavior by member organizations and an effective platform for working out differences.

2. What determines participation and defines who should join the network?

Networks that work consist of people representing organizations and institutions who share some degree of pre-existing relationship with one another. The character of pre-existing relationships may range across a wide spectrum, from loose familiarity with one another's work to a shared and contentious history, with many variations in between. Networks in the public arena form principally because members want – and often need – new kinds of relationships that will help them achieve organizational and institutional missions.

The formative stage of a network involves a peculiar sorting process as groups consider the tradeoffs between attempting to solve a big public problem on their own and the possibility of engaging with others who understand the problem, but perhaps from a differing perspective. The dance of formation needs to involve all members in a process that causes each and all to calculate the stakes they are willing to risk in joining with other organizations. This process leads to networks with the varying characteristics identified earlier as cooperative, coordinative and collaborative. Groups may find themselves considering and reconsidering the stakes and associated risks as new kinds of relationships evolve. Network members need to find ways to talk about stakes and risks candidly. They also need to know, in scoping out the scale of what they want to accomplish, their tolerance for opening network membership to other groups they may see as important to the effort. Will the network expand its reach by accepting new members? Under what circumstances and on what terms? Groups will join networks for a variety of reasons, and they may choose to stay engaged for new reasons they can only discover once they have agreed to and lived with the commitments expected of participants.

3. How firm is member commitment to this network?

Once networks organize around and define the terms of engagement and a compelling shared purpose, member commitment to the network must remain firm or the network risks weakness and drift. As member organizations designate representatives to the network, they must also make success in the network setting part of the representative's formal job description. The weight of each representative's decision making authority in his or her home organization often indicates the organization's larger commitment to the network and its purpose. Representing a member organization in a network is serious business, not at all a duty tossed to just any manager or deputy. In making agreements, deliberating issues, negotiating interests, confirming information or taking action, a representative's need to consult or confer with the member organization will speed up or slow down the network's progress. A representative's authority should be commensurate with the issues the network is addressing; the higher the stakes, the higher the representative's authority needs be. One rule of thumb: any network agreement carries only as much authority and weight as the people who make and sign the agreement carry in their own institution. Organizations should be committed to a network from the top and should view their representatives' participation in the network as if the organization's success at home hangs in the balance. Absent such a robust commitment, after all, what's the point of wasting a representative's time and the time of other organizations?

4. To what extent does the network have continuous outside support or sponsorship?

When previously unaffiliated groups make the decision to organize as a network, it speaks volumes about each group's determination to address a public problem in new ways. Still, outside political, civic or institutional support – sometimes called "sponsorship" or "civic sanction" – can make a decisive difference in network effectiveness. Sometimes that sponsorship may come from local elected leaders or prestigious individuals with broad civic, governmental, labor or business sector stature. Carefully assess and enlist outside support with sufficient clout to make sure the network has, from the start, the greatest promise for sustainability. Some networks acknowledge sponsorship support by creating advisory groups; some prefer their sponsors – and the sponsors prefer it as well – to stay low key and out of full public view.

5. How do we determine and organize our action priorities?

Determining priorities begins even as representatives move toward clarity about the network purpose. Members rank action priorities around their relative urgency, importance and estimated timeframe needed for resolution. Priorities should emerge from a measured, respectful exploration of member interests and areas of alignment. The process must allow both time and safe space in which members can voice and clarify what each finds essential to achieving the network's purpose from the vantage point of their particular mission.

Because groups establish public interest networks in response to large-scale issues, representatives need to realize that fluid factors in the external environment require networks to remain nimble in reorganizing priorities. Sudden or even gradual shifts in the political, social or economic environment require agility and responsiveness on the part of network members. Groups need to appreciate that a network setting in which members decide to flex and respond nimbly can move more easily within the dynamics of public policy and politics. Network representatives must keep abreast of evolving conditions and build space in the network to share perspectives, shift focus when desirable and evaluate the impact of their efforts on advancing the network's purpose.

Carefully assess and enlist outside support with sufficient clout to make sure the network has, from the start, the greatest promise for sustainability.

Network priorities often become the focus of work groups, active subsets of members who focus on essential activities responsive to agreed-upon priorities and who maintain an open line of communication back to the entire network. (Work groups are discussed in detail on page 61.)

The following chart provides an orientation to two fundamentally different management perspectives. Understanding these perspectives is critical to distinguishing between the management demands of an organization and those of a network. Most people who lead, run and work in organizations readily understand the features of the "classic organizational perspective" described in the chart. This is because it is the typical management structure used in organizing businesses, nonprofits and governmental agencies and institutions. The "network perspective" on management is less well understood and requires people who work in traditional settings to adopt a new frame of reference when thinking about network management.

Two Perspectives on Management

PERSPECTIVES

DIMENSIONS

	Classic Organizational Perspective	**Network Perspective**
Organizational Setting	Single authority structure	Divided authority structure
Goal Structure	Activities guided by clear goals and well-defined problems	Various and changing definition of problems and goals
Role of Manager	System controller	Mediator, process manager and network builder
Management Tasks	Planning and guiding organizational processes	Guiding interactions and providing opportunities
Management Activities	Planning, designing and leading	Selecting actors and resources, influencing network conditions and handling strategic complexity

From W. J. M. Kickert, E.-H. Klijn and J. F. M. Koppenjan, *Managing Complex Networks: Strategies for the Public Sector.* (London, England: Sage Publications, 1997). Reprinted with permission from publisher.

6. How will we organize, manage and govern the network?

Networks operate not on the basis of single-authority hierarchies (as do most individual organizations), but rather on the basis of equal partnership and divided-authority structures. Equal partnership and divided-authority structures require profound mutual respect for the autonomy, interests, voice and effectiveness of each organization or institution committed to the network and its purpose. And every network will define equal partnership somewhat differently. Equal does not need to mean, for example, that every member organization has similar assets, political connections or fundraising clout. Nevertheless, members in all vital, active networks likely will seek to influence one another in various ways. Networks have distinct political features with complex inter-organizational dynamics, deeply valued interests, a mixture of highly motivated personalities and members with constituencies that need satisfying. Successful network politics are more likely to come from members working to persuade one another based on the merits of shared interests rather than on their dominating size, economic clout, political muscle, social or civic status and other distinctions.

Network members can model themselves upon a variety of organizing structures or create hybrid forms of their own. Possibilities include:

- Self-governing general assembly with team structures. Members function by making purpose and priority decisions as a general assembly; teams in the form of "work groups" or "action groups" take on tasks and activities related to advancing network priorities; and members select and hold accountable a small coordinating group responsible for administrative matters such as developing budgets, managing finances and serving as a reporting group for employees or contractors. This structure may – but not necessarily – require the convenience and advantages that come with the legal form of a tax-exempt, public benefit corporation. Alternatively, the capacities and potentially valuable neutrality of a tax-exempt, fiscal sponsoring organization may be of greatest benefit. Examples include: Community Partners in Los Angeles, Tides Center in San Francisco, Colorado Nonprofit Development Center in Denver or Third Sector New England in Boston.

- Lead organization structure. In this approach, one member organization or institution is nominally "in charge," but the overriding terms of equal partnership must still apply or risk threatening the network's integrity and the ability of network members to work together on an even playing field. The lead organization cannot singly determine the network's purpose nor direct the decisions, establish the priorities or assign the tasks and activities of the network. Rather, the lead organization takes responsibility – perhaps as all or part of its in-kind resource commitment to the network – for certain operational, financial and administrative aspects of the network, effectively extending an umbrella of fiscal and corporate "sponsorship," while allowing the network members to self-govern and control their own agenda and work. Network members may enter into a separate side agreement with the lead organization detailing the terms of the lead organization's role, responsibilities and resource commitment. Alternatively, members can incorporate details of the lead organization's roles, responsibilities and boundaries directly into the written network agreement (discussed in detail later).

- Network manager structure. Able to integrate neatly with either or both of the previous two approaches, the network selects someone to function as the network manager. Because of the position's pivotal importance, the choice of network manager requires full concurrence – and utter confidence – from all members of a network. Different networks title the role in different ways; common names besides network manager include administrator, coordinator, executive secretary or facilitator. The terms "director" or "executive director," though used in some networks, connote a role more apt for single-authority, classic organization structures rather than the non-hierarchical (and therefore non-"directive") conditions preferred in network settings. The roles played by network managers differ significantly from those played by the executive directors and line managers of classic organizations. Network managers understand and navigate the complex relationships among members over whom they have no directive power. Rather, the network manager seeks to recognize and help members capitalize on opportunities, clarify member interests, identify conflicts, facilitate communication, maximize available resources, mediate differences and influence the network's capacity to fulfill its purpose. Strong network managers don't just know all of their members' interests and organizations exceedingly well, they are masters at handling strategic complexity with cool and calm, using tools that anticipate and resolve conflict – and they always keep their own egos in proper check and the interests of the network in the foreground.

A network manager receives supervision from the members, sometimes through a small coordinating committee but always accountable to the whole. Network governance becomes the collective obligation of all network members working together around their agreed-upon purpose, priorities, tasks and activities and counting on the network manager to facilitate a smooth flow. In a network setting, very different from classic organizations, no "board of directors" sets policy, approves plans and sits back waiting for the network manager and a large staff to see the plans through to execution. With exceptions, of course, like the United Nations (one of Earth's largest and most complex collaborative networks!), most networks have small numbers of paid personnel and perhaps occasional consultants to conduct work. This means that tasks and activities agreed on by network members frequently need the commitment of member organization resources such as lent staff time to get things done.

Strong network managers... are masters at handling strategic complexity with cool and calm.

7. What methods will we use to establish new relationships?

Recognizing the importance of forming new relationships often motivates the creation of networks or follows quickly on the heels of organizing one. The work of forming new relationships means members need a variety of formal and informal processes to strengthen and deepen the essential bonds of trust necessary for the network to succeed. Too easily dismissed as "touchy-feely," relationship-building – as this book and the experience of network participants shows time and again – lies at the core of effective networks.

Some useful informal relationship-building methods that can shape and change members' perceptions about one another include simple things like shared meals, organized social events and time together in non-network settings. Some networks rotate meetings among member organizations to better acquaint themselves with the sights, sounds, feel and working realities of different network member workplaces. Structured team- and trust-building activities for network members (such as ropes courses, specialized skill trainings or briefings from successful outside networks) can re-orient member relationship assumptions. Other activities that help set power differences aside can aid members in seeing one another as individual, complicated human beings, a skill that helps as much when negotiating interests on difficult tasks as it does in making the network's equal partnership more pleasant. Day-long or extended trips to places that reflect members' common civic or community interests can also offer both formal and informal opportunities for new relationships – not to mention new knowledge and insight – to develop.

Rotate meetings among member organizations to better [understand] the sights, sounds, feel and working realities of different network member workplaces.

Formal methods that establish and integrate rules, roles, responsibilities and routines into the network can range widely. Some examples include:

- Establish expectations for standards of conduct. Groups work better when, at the outset, members set basic ground rules for norms of conduct. Such rules tend to work best when they assume mutual tolerance, common civility and include a healthy dose of generosity – particularly when anticipating the inevitable, though often productive, conflicts or debates that attend networked action. Sanctions for violating standards of conduct, however, should be spelled out in advance and upheld by the group.

- ADOPT AND USE EFFECTIVE MEETING METHODS. Written material and real-time trainings abound in how to set up, manage and run effective meetings. *How to Make Meetings Work* by Doyle and Strauss (1993) provides an evergreen source of wisdom. Since much network activity will revolve around face-to-face interaction in both small and large groups, identifying and investing time in learning meeting techniques will pay off in efficiency and results. Any network that hires a manager must include meeting facilitation skills in the manager's job description.

- ADOPT PROVEN DECISION MAKING TECHNIQUES. Arriving at agreement can take time. Skilled meeting facilitators and managers know many techniques for helping groups consider and make decisions. Simple, effective techniques (such as those taught by Sam Kaner, Ph.D., and the trainers from California-based Community at Work) can help groups in everything from efficiently completing routine business to negotiating difficult issues, while minimizing frustration and sore feelings. Network members generally find "majority rules" unacceptable for decisions because of the potential for leaving out the concerns of so many members. Some networks prefer to operate by allowing negotiated consensus to develop slowly over time. Some might seek and act on the recommended course of action from work groups, from groups organized around particular interests, or even from special ad hoc task forces comprised of members and even augmented by people with special content knowledge.

- Adopt proven conflict resolution methods. As discussed later in this chapter, groups need to anticipate and surface conflicts and meet them with proven methods of dispute resolution. Disputes can arise for many reasons, both complex and simple. For example, high stakes may be on the line over scarce resources when a network has set itself up to bring about fundamental system change, as did Sacramento's Water Forum. There, the group adopted a robust "interest-based negotiation" method of conflict resolution, a deliberative process in which all network members' respective interests were aired and fairly weighed.

  Training and practice in such techniques of dispute resolution are not required for network members who are simply grappling with how to cooperate in a joint conference or symposium. Generally, in these situations, good common-sense, give-and-take consensus techniques using respectful discussion and compromise can get everyone to "yes." One simple rule of thumb for successful networks is to fit the robustness of their chosen methods of handling disputes to the intensity of the stakes and risks that brought the network members together in the first place. Success requires agreeing about what type of technique to use and remaining open to discovering new techniques as the network evolves. Train all members in how the network prefers to approach decisions and resolve issues and orient new network members as they come aboard. All networks need to routinely review the forms of conflict resolution – in place or available – that will support the network in achieving its purpose.

8. How will we conduct our work?

Operational nuts and bolts will evolve over time as the network hones its focus, develops momentum and starts producing the results desired by its members. In a network, work is the operative syllable. Networks achieve meaning and form through the common ground work members identify and agree on. Overly constraining forms of planning inhibit or delay getting to the work. Yes, members need to sort out the network structure and governance, but that becomes part of the work, too, and it will evolve as members see results and understand in action the complexity of their undertaking.

A simple planning outline in a network may include only a few elements within which to make decisions: purpose, priorities, tasks and activities. The customary struggles with vision and mission statements, by-laws, complicated board governance structures, voting procedures, committee assignments and other such trappings of classically structured organizations will divert precious member attention and energy. Case studies demonstrate newly formed networks can work from a strong unifying purpose, agreement about priority areas of focus and a few simple structures that will foster greater efficiency and facilitate immediate action. A few examples of structures in which members can contain various tasks and activities include:

- INTEREST GROUPS. Interest groups – subsets of members with similar perspectives – serve as one means for members to organize themselves and conduct work. Open interest group meetings, accessible and transparent to all network members, build trust and understanding across the network. Members listen as they each surface and compare the issues that matter most to them.

- WORK GROUPS. Also referred to as task groups or action groups, work groups are another means of developing, refining and addressing network priorities. A cross-section of the general network membership, these small groups are often formed at open meetings to provide space for members to delve more deeply into issues, sort through what work they need to do and divide up responsibilities for getting it done. Often, this involves committing the resources (money, staff, time) of various member organizations. Other times, network members may agree to jointly raise funds or contribute resources from their own organizational coffers. Staff or consultant time paid for with these resources can then be divided up among work groups to support members in certain tasks and activities. Work groups allow members to sustain a dialogue, share the results of work in progress, better understand each other and align their efforts.

Between general assemblies, work group progress will invariably benefit from all modes of communication and gathering including periodic conference calls, small group meetings, extended retreats or web conferences. The timing and frequency of work group meetings varies. A work group monitoring the latest academic research of interest to the entire network membership or monitoring a study the network has chosen to fund may meet or confer as new research surfaces or as the study hits certain milestones and researchers need to check in. A public policy work group keeping track of fast-moving bills during a legislative session might meet frequently to keep tabs on elected officials' positions and strategize how to assert network member (collective and/or individual) influence.

- COORDINATING AND ADMINISTRATIVE OVERSIGHT GROUPS. A small coordination group will facilitate the mundane but necessary administrative and operational tasks that keep a network running smoothly. These tasks might involve network budgeting, handling finances, executing employment agreements or contracts with staff or consultants, or coordinating periodic reviews. Such a group might also help the whole network gauge progress within work groups. If the network has a paid manager, the members of this group and the manager work closely together. The group derives its authority entirely from the consent of all the network members and remains fully accountable to them. This subset or committee should handle money matters with the utmost transparency and discretion. Note that this group has no governance or directive authority over the network or its members. The committee is explicitly not "in charge," makes no determination of network priorities and is in place because coordination and administrative oversight help advance all the other substantive work that brought members together in the first place.

- GENERAL ASSEMBLIES. Networks need ways in which all members can gather for formal work, such as governance decision making, review and adjustment of network priorities, ratification and modification of network member agreements, progress reports from work groups, and initiation and briefing of new members. Scheduled and predictable general assemblies – the number, timing and frequency of which depend on network member preferences, size of the network, geographic issues and other factors – are ideal gathering places through which to make progress. Most networks quickly develop routines around their meetings. Frequency depends on the kinds and urgency of issues at hand. Regular assemblies of the entire membership produce the greatest results if members meet in between these sessions as part of smaller work groups. The regular assembly, set up to hear reports from work groups and then serve as a forum for debate, discussion and decisions, can prove extraordinarily productive, not to mention invigorating to members. General sessions may use a standard agenda of routine items but should allow flexible room for new issues warranting network attention.

9. What kind of agreement should we make to function as a network?

Network members generally want the confidence, common "memory" and sense of completion that comes with a written document reflecting their mutual, voluntary participation in the network. Variously referred to as memoranda of understanding, compacts, charters, relational contracts or, simply, agreements, these documents reflect the decisions made on the range of matters discussed in the previous section. Depending on the network's purpose, the agreement may address a range of other needs or concerns that arise in the process of establishing the network. Written agreements, whatever term members use to describe them, serve as a continuous reference point as the network embarks on its activities. They can provide a way of orienting or presenting the network to other interested audiences. Signing the agreement is also a means for new members to demonstrate their understanding of and commitment to an existing network.

Network agreements are living documents. They should be detailed enough to document and guide decisions as the network pursues its purpose, and yet broad enough to stand the test of incremental changes that will inevitably come with time. Agreements should be considered periodically and their provisions reconsidered in light of new, evolving network conditions and realities.

No single network agreement model exists because all networks are unique. However, depending on the type of network, agreements should address at least the following elements:

- *Reasons for the network agreement,* detailing the background and history that led to the network's creation.
- *Statement and description of network purpose,* perhaps describing the circumstances members experienced that led them to join in common cause.
- *Statement of shared values or principles,* including detail sufficient enough that members can distinguish the unique interests they share in common.
- *Current network priorities and focus of critical work,* recognizing that priorities will receive considered review and may shift over time.

- *Membership,* including list of establishing members, a profile of member qualifications and guidelines for member entry and exit (voluntary or otherwise).
- *Roles, responsibilities and required commitments of members,* including details of funding and other resource or service contribution obligations.
- *Governance structure,* including composition of the oversight or administrative committee and meeting and decision making procedures.
- *Operational structure,* including structural details related to work groups, systems of accountability and conflict resolution.
- *Role of network staff,* consultants and other supporters, including a network manager job description (see Appendix F).
- *Funding and resources,* including "self-taxing" arrangements, thoughtful and careful procedures for seeking funds from outside sources and a preliminary budget.

No single network agreement model exists because all networks are unique.

The examples discussed in the appendices of this book provide practical illustrations of networks in action and links to organizational web sites, including to some actual examples of network agreements. Sample templates for a Network Manager job description and a Network Agreement have also been provided in Appendices F and G.

10. How do network members hold themselves and one another accountable?

Because networks in no way coerce members to join, their members voluntarily – rather than legally – enforce network agreements. The agreements represent a voluntary set of commitments made by members who can decide at any time to leave the network and not fulfill future commitments spelled out in the agreement. However, if the agreement represents every member's basic interests openly and honestly negotiated, then little reason exists for groups to leave the network – unless community, economic or social conditions change sufficiently to require a fundamental reconsideration of the network purpose, structure and member composition. High member turnover, low rates of participation by network representatives or a continual "impasse" on important issues and decisions should raise a giant red flag for members.

Networks may experience instances in which one member or group of members with similar interests feels the "other guys" are not living up to the letter or spirit of the agreement. Approached as an opportunity, these trials can result in continued or voluntarily re-opened interest negotiations, new understandings among members and modifications of the network agreement. Every agreement needs some flexibility since conditions may change. Representatives from a member organization may leave their positions and new representatives may need a careful orientation to get up to speed. The more the signatories to the agreement keep each other honest and keep one another talking, the more the agreement becomes self-enforcing and the more likely issues can be resolved with additional negotiation.

11. How will we resolve conflicts?

Network participants should keep two key points in mind when dealing with conflict in any type of network. First, conflict comes with the territory and should not be avoided or pushed under the rug. Managing conflict is essential, and conflict handled skillfully can produce new ideas and synergy. Second, the capacity of network participants to deal with conflict depends upon the quality of trust shared among the members. No matter what the issue, network members will find an inescapable correlation between effective conflict resolution and trusting relationships. This makes engaging in activities, tasks and behaviors that strengthen and deepen relationships a key feature of successful networks. In addition, especially in coordinating and collaborating networks, participants must envision, negotiate and build fundamentally new types of relationships – ones that mirror and support the symphony they want to achieve between organizations (or the larger, more complex system reforms at the heart of their network's purpose).

Alongside tried and true informal methods for enhancing human relations, like social events and breaking bread, participants in networks use varied methods to address and resolve conflict. Here are some examples:

- STRUCTURED TRAINING SESSIONS IN INTER-PROFESSIONAL LEADERSHIP. Here participants learn new theories, develop a shared language and skills and potentially unlearn old or outmoded behaviors. This method was used by a network called the Service Integration Project, and the details can be found in the article, "Network Structures: Working Differently and Changing Expectations," by Keast, Mandell, Brown and Woolcock (2004).

- STRUCTURED TRAINING SESSIONS ON NON-CONFRONTATIONAL NEGOTIATING METHODS. In this approach, sometimes called "interest-based negotiation," participants surface and discuss their underlying interests, rather than their positions on issues in conflict, as a means of finding and establishing common ground. Every member organization or institution that participates in Sacramento's Water Forum (discussed on pages 46-47 and in Appendix E) trains in the skills of interest-based negotiation, and the method is routinely employed in resolving or avoiding conflict.

High member turnover, low rates of participation by network representatives or a continual "impasse" on important issues and decisions should raise a giant red flag for members.

- DEVELOPING AND SIGNING FORMAL AGREEMENTS that spell out participants' understanding of their roles and responsibilities in the network. Also referred to as relational contracts (discussed on pages 61-62 and and in Appendix G), more is available on this method in the article "Consensus Building as Role Playing and Bricolage," by Innes and Booher (1991).

- FACILITATED CONSENSUS-BUILDING DISCUSSIONS that allow all participants to be heard and encourage respectful and open-ended dialogue. Some networks routinely tap the services of outside facilitators with skill in moving groups through conflict toward compromise and agreement. Similarly, groups may draw on the skills of trusted individuals within the group to employ methods of problem solving or conflict resolution previously agreed to by members of the network. Some methods that have been used to achieve this involve scenario building, storytelling and role-playing. Innes & Booher, mentioned above, discuss this in the same article.

- INDEPENDENTLY CONDUCTED AND REPORTED FACT-FINDING RESEARCH invited by network members. This compels network members to consider and learn about the larger factual picture surrounding the systems in which they operate and around issues in conflict. From this, presumably, they can achieve a better understanding upon which to frame views and seek network-based solutions.

- AGREEING IN ADVANCE TO COMPLETE TRANSPARENCY about certain sensitive matters. One California-based network with nine organizational members dealt with the potential for conflict over approaching funding sources by agreeing to document and share with one another contacts with funders, proposals sent and the content of the proposals. This reduced the possibility for embarrassing encounters with funders, made the nine organizations intimately familiar with one another's work and opened the door for new kinds of cooperation on projects of mutual interest.

- GATHERING STAFF FROM DIFFERENT NETWORK MEMBER ORGANIZATIONS AND CO-LOCATING in offices or other settings either permanently or temporarily. Here, network members can more easily learn from one another and use this knowledge to advise their respective organizations. Exchanges of ideas, information and relationships among co-locating staff smooth communication and speed its flow, potentially defusing conflicts before they arise. The location may be within a member organization's existing space and dedicated to the network, or it may be a new site.

In many of the above examples, outside consultants, trainers or facilitators may provide skill acquisition support to network participants. Sometimes network members who are practiced in a particular approach to conflict resolution train other network members. While outside counsel is not absolutely necessary, network participants can sometimes more effectively pursue their common purpose in the presence of resource people adept at establishing a supportive and productive group atmosphere. Few network members will argue against the value of having available people skilled in helping point out and balance differentials in power, persuasion techniques, cultural assertiveness or reticence, and public speaking confidence or capability.

12. What funding and other resources will the network need, and where will the support come from?

Network members must think creatively and carefully about how to identify, tap and deploy various resource streams. The following valuable approaches can be used alone or in combination, including:

- FUNDING THROUGH MEMBER CASH CONTRIBUTIONS. Beyond commitment to the network purpose and regular participation in network tasks and activities, members may decide to fund the network through financial "self-assessment." Self-assessment means supplying funds – cash money! – from individual organizations to finance network operations. Such a funding method can provide network members with certainty and a sense of collective control over the network. Self-assessment formulas and agreements need to offer budgeting predictability for members, cover some or all of the costs of network operations, include mechanisms for periodic review and foster a sense of equity. For example, in 2010 the National Network of Fiscal Sponsors (NNFS) established a three-tier self-assessment scheme to fund a part-time coordinator and other costs to support the network. Groups were placed into tiers based on their annual operating budgets; groups with larger budgets contributed larger amounts and those with smaller budgets contributed less. The NNFS member groups, having formed a cooperating network, agreed to assess the results of their joint work regularly to determine if the self-assessment achieved what everyone expected.

Network schemes can clarify in a direct and visible way member commitmentt to the network's success. They also focus member attention on the network and help members ascribe tangible value to desired network results. To funders looking in from the outside and thinking about funding a network project, task or activity, or even certain network operational expenses, a self-assessment system can provide reassurance that members highly value working together. Funders can readily see that network members care enough to place their own money on the line in service to the network's shared purpose.

To funders looking in from the outside and thinking about funding a network project, task or activity, or even certain network operational expenses, a self-assessment system can provide reassurance that members highly value working together.

- SUPPORT THROUGH MEMBER IN-KIND CONTRIBUTIONS. In-kind contributions of staff time and expertise, office space, materials and services (such as postage, printing, copying and telephones) that would otherwise require raising funds are another form of self- assessment. Like commitments of cash, in-kind contributions represent tangible investments by members in the success of the network. They also sharpen each contributing member's ownership of network results.

- GRANT SEEKING FOR GENERAL OPERATIONS. Networks may choose to approach various donors such as individuals or private, corporate or community foundations for general operating funds over extended time frames, usually best measured in years. The Water Forum, for example, receives funding largely allocated by city and county government agencies. The most likely funders will be those predisposed to understand the leverage that networked action can provide to their grant funds. Short-term, start-up grants can be useful, but networks that launch a long-term agenda with only short-term funding and no other means of support risk early collapse and failure.

- GRANT SEEKING FOR PROJECT ACTIVITIES. Networks that achieve early and visible gains may find themselves sufficiently credible to qualify for project grants in areas important to accomplishing the network's purpose and of interest to particular funders. For example, networks that form action groups involved in working through compelling issues (related to the network's larger purpose) may attract "project" or "work group" grants that the network can administer. Budgeting for any project grant should include line items to cover a fair share of staffing and administering the network.

Before seeking grants for joint work, members of a network need to be clear, transparent and in agreement with one another about the sources and uses of any funds applied for and received to conduct joint work. For example, an advocacy coordination network known as

Californians for Pesticide Reform (CPR) (they think of themselves as a "coalition") goes to great lengths to assure a high level of financial transparency and documentation of all member interactions with funders. CPR members refer to this as their "non-compete agreement," which requires that all decisions about approaching funders for grants specifically within CPR's purpose – pesticide reform advocacy in California – must be discussed and jointly agreed upon by the CPR steering committee. Members have developed sufficient trust to share this information, confident that jointly approaching certain funders for network tasks and activities does not preclude them from approaching the same or similar funders for ongoing operations of their individual organizations. Most funders know the network well enough to appreciate the care with which network members go about deciding when a joint approach for funding makes better sense than one organization going alone, or, more confusing, many organizations approaching a funder to support the same project.

Choices about the sources, stability and duration of network funding cannot be taken lightly. Member-funded networks will carry with them as many, though perhaps different, expectations about network accountability as will externally funded networks. All funders have expectations that the money they commit to an effort will produce tangible, even measurable results. It should come as no surprise to network participants that funders may want to influence grantee agendas, attach explicit or implicit grant performance expectations or enjoy privileged access to network deliberations. Such expectations imposed from funders who are not actually members of the network, yet seek to influence its work, cannot be pushed aside. They represent a potential source of conflict, which must be confronted squarely in networks. Network members need to anticipate and plan how they will manage funder expectations long before those expectations arise.

Maximum flexibility should be a network watchword that guides decisions about accepting any funding from any source. Networks should develop a healthy preference for driving their own agenda, even waiting to present the network plan in a relatively advanced state of development to outside funders. In negotiating start-up or ongoing support, network leaders should avoid agreeing to funding terms that skew the network agenda away from the stated network purpose. The extreme situation of a network purpose being co-opted by the chase for cash is discussed more fully below.

If necessary, members may want to decide whether outside funders meet the requirements for membership. If funders do not qualify, network members always have the option of offering them special status, perhaps as welcome observers and occasional advisors. Networks funded with public tax monies from city, county, special district, state or federal sources may need to comply with legal requirements for transparency and open meetings.

13. What are the challenges of funder-driven networks?

One recurrent problem that networks encounter involves a dilemma that places their integrity in jeopardy from the start. Networks often form solely at the impetus of outside funders. The funder's dollars – along with implicit or explicit expectations – dictate and too often narrowly circumscribe network possibilities. Though network members tempted into this bind can acquire bad cases of denial, their driving network purpose frequently boils down to "keep the funder happy to sustain the flow of cash."

For example, top leaders of several organizations doing similar work across Los Angeles agreed to participate in several sub-regional cooperative networks because a large funder wanted to see them jointly build service capacity. Once funding contracts were signed, however, many of the top leaders handed responsibility for compliance to mid-level managers, ignoring the importance of helping managers navigate inter-organizational, relationship-building challenges. In the process, leaders lost touch with the potential synergistic value that might result from their managers and case workers allying cross-organizationally for wider service impact with teams from similar sub-regional organizations. The funder sensed problems in this approach to forming networks when they saw their network grantees merely complying with certain funding requirements, such as periodic staff gatherings, rather than using the effort and the funder's resource grants as a springboard to greater impact. Despite large expenditures on technical assistance and outside resource intervention, the funder's vision was never realized. Members of most of the networks ended their contracts with little or nothing to show for the effort, including no internalized will to continue cooperating after the funding initiative ended.

Groups chasing network funding offered up by funders (because the funders insist that the groups cooperate as

All funders have expectations that the money they commit to an effort will produce tangible, even measurable results.

a grant condition) simply perpetuate cynical patterns endemic to the competitive economy of the nonprofit sector. Nonprofit leaders, not to mention the people their organizations serve, benefit when they can honestly recognize and wisely resist this short-term, grab-what-you-can behavior. Funders can avoid wasting grant dollars by resisting the temptation to undertake initiatives imposing requirements for inter-organizational collaboration by groups without pre-existing relationships – one of the fundamental underpinnings of successful networked action. Funders who look for sound evidence that groups have had prior relationships – even if those relationships have been troubled or tense, but show signs of potential resolution – stand a better chance of funding successful networks. Funders who craft grant guidelines that ignore the importance of pre-existing relationships risk creating perverse incentives. These incentives often cause "Potemkin" networks to arise that have the outward appearance of groups joined in common cause, but no internal substance, integrity or lasting desire among the partners to work together. Sharp-eyed nonprofit leaders ever on the lookout for resources have a habit of performing empty rituals of inter-group commitment without a genuine shared purpose. If funders fail to dig deeply into the quality, character and history of relationships among organizations in whose networks they invest, the funders have no reason to expect strong, transformative networks as a result.

14. What other key resources do we need to have in place?

Other necessary resources to have in place include

administrative support to facilitate network management and coordination, outside professional counsel and, most important, the time and participation of designated member organization representatives.

- ADMINISTRATIVE SUPPORT. Administrative support activities and requirements range widely. They may include handling meeting logistics, keeping and maintaining network records, summarizing notes from work group meetings, managing and updating databases or websites, printing and distributing reports and materials, answering phone queries, and coordinating the details and meeting agendas when network members periodically convene. Network members may decide to include administrative support personnel as part of the overall network budget. Alternatively, one or more members, as part of an in-kind contribution to the network, may dedicate part- or full-time administrative support to meet network needs. The National Network for Fiscal Sponsors, for example, allocates part of its self-assessment funding to pay for part of a staff person's time who already works at one of the NNFS member organizations.

Members need to value the network highly enough to where the argument of "we all have other jobs in our own organizations" changes to "what we accomplish in the network makes my organization more successful."

- OUTSIDE PROFESSIONAL EXPERTISE. Depending on what the network intends to accomplish, addressing network priorities may require various sorts of outside professional expertise. Some networks may want to commission a consulting firm to conduct independent research to gather facts and provide analysis on topics of concern. Others may want to strengthen themselves in areas where collective member expertise is missing or weak. As discussed earlier, network members may realize they need training or skilled counsel in resolving conflicts and disputes. To the extent that a network may need outside professional expertise, network members need to agree to the task or activity the expert will perform.

- TIME AND ENGAGED PARTICIPATION. Member representatives to the network must allow sufficient time for the kinds of engagement that lead to trusting relationships and advance the network purpose. This most critical of resources comes with a price – time away from other activities in their own organization – and cannot be undervalued. Still, if network participation stands any chance of enabling member groups to effectively pursue their common purpose in ways that better fulfill individual organization missions, the time spent "in network" should prove worth the investment. Members need to value the network highly enough to where the argument of "we all have other jobs in our own organizations" changes to "what we accomplish in the network makes my organization more successful." One concrete way to assure this happens is for the network agreement to state – and every network member organization agree – that the job description of any person designated to serve as a member representative has the network representation duty spelled out as a responsibility in their formal job description.

Chapter 4

What to Watch as your Network Works

As discussed earlier, groups organizing into networks will always encounter and need to overcome obstacles, challenges and difficulties. Network organizers can hurt their own credibility and damage relationships with prospective network members by leading them to believe that working in a multi-organizational setting will be free of problems. In reality, networks mean greater complexity for inter-organizational relationships. Forming the network – and all that forming and governing the network entails – needs to be the better tradeoff when compared to the usual business of organizations operating completely independent from one another. (See chart on following page.)

Forming the network...needs to be the better tradeoff when compared to [business as usual].

Even when groups tackle and overcome the conflicts that arise in the creation of a network, issues will continue to arise. Members participating in a network will find themselves defaulting to traditional roles with which they feel comfortable and successful in their own organizations. For example, although they may intellectually understand and accept that "no one is in charge" in a network, some members may cling to a desire to assert both personality and power as if they can take charge and "direct" the focus of the network.

When to Form a Network

- Problems are complex and potential solutions lie with many public agencies, organizations, programs and services. No single agency or two can approach the problem.
- Top administrators/decision makers recognize the complexity of the problem and are willing to lend their resources, e.g., financial support and staff.
- Problems have no or few readily apparent and/or feasible solutions. They have to be worked out by several parties.
- Resources to address problems - such as time, money, expertise, information, legitimacy and status - can be gained from the combination of entities.
- Participants have the ability to manage uncertainty and solve complex problems.
- Participants recognize the opportunity to learn, adapt and develop new competencies and new approaches to problems.
- Participants are willing to share costs and associated risks of new problem solutions, programs and service approaches.
- Potential influence can be gained over policy/program domain, competitive positioning for the problem areas and new clients.
- Rapid and efficient responses can be jointly developed to address changing demands brought on by the introduction of new technologies.
- Participants are willing to explore new approaches and methods.
- Participants are willing to engage in constructive, deliberative dialogue/engagement that leads to the development of new possibilities.
- Participants are willing to confront and manage potential conflict-generating issues.
- Participants are willing to treat all as equals, regardless of one's hierarchical position in the home agency.
- Key partners are willing to commit to a long-term process that involves reframing issues into new perspectives.
- Participants are willing to align services and programs that impact others.

Adapted from Robert Agranoff, Presentation at the Office of the U.S. Director of National Intelligence, NetCentric Leadership Conference. (Herndon, VA, June 2007).

If these behaviors result in dominance or distortion of the network purpose by one or a few network members, then network members need to step up and re-examine the assumptions that brought them together in the first place. All members need to be fully aware of the natural human tendency to revert to the more comfortable "directive" roles their own organizational settings demand. This awareness can lead members to find new ways of fostering relationships as equal partners with other network members.

It will serve network members well to remember a fundamental difference between classic organizations and networks comprised of many organizations working together. In classic organizations, leaders work hard to push conflict down to its appropriate managerial level and expect managers to resolve the conflict and feed solutions upward. In networks, since typically no managerial "levels" exist, members must govern from a posture of equal partnership with a continual awareness of the natural conflicts about interests, turf, power, competitive position and other issues that invariably occur between organizations.

Members need to maintain a high level of vigilance even as they pursue the network's agreed-upon priorities and pursue network tasks and activities.

Successful networks establish an enlightened process from the outset of identifying and anticipating where conflicts most likely will arise. Depending on the predicted intensity of various potential conflicts, the network members then establish in advance the ways they will recognize when they have entered a conflict zone and the process they plan to use for working through the conflict to restore common ground. In this way, groups start by acknowledging the fact that conflict is a natural by-product of working in complex organizational settings and commit themselves to dealing with conflict in ways that do not derail the possibilities of progress in areas where groups have agreement. For example, members of The Water Forum decided that because the network membership represented four distinctive areas of interest – water agencies, environmental groups, governments and developers – and because high stakes and risky trade-offs would always be involved when making decisions, they needed a robust and highly structured process of "interest-based negotiation." Less complicated networks require less complicated conflict management processes and different kinds of vigilance about changing network conditions.

Monitoring Progress and Maintaining Continuity

Because a range of both internal and external developments can influence conditions in the network, members need to maintain a high level of vigilance even as they pursue the network's agreed-upon priorities and pursue network tasks and activities.

The questions in this section can help members stay alert to what's happening in the network setting.

Assessing and Tracking Progress

- What have we tangibly accomplished toward fulfilling our purpose as a network that individual member organizations and institutions could not have accomplished alone?

- How have the people served by our network members benefited as a result of changes we have created or influenced through the network's action?
- How have relationships among members of the network changed?
- How have the workings of each member organization changed as a result of participation in the network?

Continuity of Network Purpose

- Has the network's purpose changed?
- If so, is there agreement from everyone and a full understanding of the implications?
- Does the change have an impact on the network's legitimacy?

Operational Continuity

- Has the way the network operates changed?
- What factors have led to the changes and are all members aware of and agreeable to the changes?
- What impact have operational changes had on member participation in all aspects of the network's activities?

Member Participation and Contributions

- To what extent are members participating regularly and substantively?
- To what extent are members contributing resources to the network?

- To what extent has any member's influence or contribution grown disproportionate to that of other members or otherwise altered network equilibrium?
- How have we encouraged network members to uphold their commitments to the network?
- Have we first attempted negotiations and then enforced sanctions when members have not honored their commitments?

Membership Changes

- Have we opened participation to new organizations and institutions?
- If so, how well have we oriented new members to the network's purpose, history, agreements, priorities, tasks and activities accomplished so far, methods of managing and resolving conflict, and the results we have achieved?
- Have members left the network?
- If so, what factors have influenced their decision to leave?
- What do the member departures say about the effectiveness of the network?
- What have we done to reinvigorate member commitment to the network purpose, keep our priorities current, celebrate achievements and prevent burnout?

Decision Making and Conflict Resolution Processes

- To what extent does the full membership have a concrete role in governance and making decisions?

- Has member involvement been consistent?
- What decision making processes have we found work best for us?
- What additional decision making skills and training would serve us well?
- How effective have we been at anticipating, surfacing and resolving conflicts?
- When conflicts arise, have we mined them fully for the opportunities they represent to understand one another better, find common ground for moving ahead and addressing our network purpose more effectively?
- What additional conflict resolution skills and training would serve us well?

Professor Robert Agranoff of Indiana University reviewed *Networks that Work* and helped summarize several points about why not to form a network; see chart on the following page.

Why *Not* to Form a Network

- The problems/issues are minor and can be resolved by dyadic or triadic inter-organizational contact and accommodation, thus deflating expectations.
- The focus/orientation is vague or meaningless, i.e. to coordinate some unspecified shared problems.
- Key potential partners insist on particular approaches or methods for solving problems.
- Top administrators/decision makers withhold their support or pay lip service to the endeavor.
- Top administrators/decision makers do not delegate authority to their staff to speak for their organizations.
- Potential activist administrators and specialists are unwilling to commit time, energy and resources to the undertaking.
- Key potential activists refuse to confront core conflict-producing issues and related competitive or historic tensions.
- Key partners are unable to overcome conflict, confusion and disagreement over what "problem(s)" the network is approaching.
- Key participants fail to treat one another as entirely equal partners regardless of social, political or economic strength of individual groups.
- Complications arise in communications, management or conflict resolution, resulting in dysfunctional operations.
- Expectations are that issues can be resolved in a short time frame instead of an orientation to small yet essential "wins."
- From the outset, there is a failure to reframe problems or issues, not based on participants' individual perspectives, but rather on new perspectives drawn from deliberative-based agreements.

Adapted by Robert Agranoff from Paul Vandeventer and Myrna Mandell, *Networks That Work: A Practitioner's Guide to Managing Networked Action.* (Los Angeles, CA: Community Partners, 2007), 20-22.

A Few Final Thoughts

A handful of key concepts emerge again and again in the preceding discussion about networks. They comprise a set of guiding principles that contribute to network effectiveness, productivity and vitality. They include:

- Focus on shared purpose.
- Start from pre-existing relationships.
- Make sure members assess their tolerance for risk.
- Respect organizational and institutional autonomy, even while establishing common ground to move from independence to interdependence.
- Assure up-front time, resource and organizational commitment from key players.
- Build new types of relationships.
- Emphasize equal partnership.
- Expect – even embrace – areas where conflict is likely to arise, developing practices for anticipating, surfacing and resolving it to establish common ground.
- Secure needed resources for operation without letting outside resource providers distort, deflect or diffuse the network purpose.

Incorporating these principles into the priorities, activities and management of any style of network will give rise to challenges and constraints. Remember:

- *Members must examine their organizational tolerance for participating in multi-organizational change.* Stakes and risks for members grow correspondingly higher as network ambitions grow. Risk-averse members pushed past their limits will pose a drag to an ambitious network agenda.
- *Formative processes should not trump productivity.* Members must invest time in setting up the network, agreeing on priorities and defining key tasks and activities. Yet they need to remember that the point of the network is to jointly act together – even if in simple and straightforward early-stage ways – to advance the purpose that binds them.
- *Network involvement should open up new ways of thinking rather than impose boundaries and limits to creativity.* Members benefit most when they come prepared to develop new habits of thinking both organizationally and within the network setting.
- *Single-organization settings and network settings differ fundamentally.* Members must orient themselves from the beginning – and remind themselves frequently – to distinguish the basic differences between what it takes to lead and direct an organization well and what it takes to manage, facilitate and participate productively in a network in which people at the table come from many autonomous organizations.
- *Openness to change and awareness of what's driving change go hand in hand.* Network members need to recognize and appreciate the more intangible results – beyond substantive network-driven task and activity

accomplishments – that accrue in the form of new relationships, values and perceptions.

- *Recognizing differences and tolerating them as opportunities rather than barriers can lead to productive common ground.* When leaders and staff choose to work together in network settings, they encounter at very close quarters one another's political, cultural, stylistic, behavioral, value, attitudinal and operational differences. Everyone needs to cop to that fact and own the prospect that some differences can produce annoyance, even conflict. Confronting these differences while keeping the network purpose in mind means developing new skills of focus, negotiation, compromise and group work.

When organizations succeed in joining forces for the greater good, when the shared purpose comes first, the results can exponentially exceed what any single group can achieve on its own.

These constraints notwithstanding, members need to keep in mind the potential of a network that works. When organizations succeed in joining forces for the greater good, when the shared purpose comes first, the results can exponentially exceed what any single group can achieve on its own. Indeed, addressing most large-scale public issues cannot be achieved without networked action. When networks work, everyone wins.

We hope this guide has provided you and your organization with useful tools and illustrative case studies as you consider, form and evolve your network. We encourage you to share your thoughts and experiences with us. Your feedback will help ensure that any future editions continue to reflect the most current needs and best practices of the full range of networks. Please forward comments, questions, thoughts and suggestions to networks@CommunityPartners.org.

Appendices

Network Case Studies

A Cooperating Network Example:
Southern California College Access Network

B Cooperating Network Example:
North American Alliance for Fair Employment

C Coordinating Network Example:
The Child Care Alliance of Los Angeles

D Coordinating Network Example:
The California Partnership

E Collaborating Network Example:
The Water Forum

Templates

F Position Description:
Sample Job Description for a Network Manager

G Network Agreement:
Sample Template for a Network Agreement

Bibliography

Useful Resources and Websites

Southern California College Access Network

Cooperating Network Example

The Issue

The Southern California College Access Network (SoCal CAN) is an alliance of 37 community-based organizations working to promote a college-going and completion culture in Los Angeles County. SoCal CAN members provide direct support to low-income students and families to ensure they are academically, financially and socially prepared to go to and through college. Together, SoCal CAN members have assisted more than 45,000 students, with the vast majority being the first in their family to attend college.

Formed in 2005, the network regularly convenes leaders and program staff from member organizations to share promising practices, develop common tools, build strategic partnerships, leverage resources and lend a collective voice to policy discussions impacting college access and success. A three-person network management team facilitates convenings, communication, cooperative problem-solving efforts, joint program development and the connectivity of existing services and resources.

The Challenges

- Policy advocacy is a new area of work for the network. While members share the common goal of making college-going and completion accessible to all, prioritizing a policy agenda is challenging.

- Connecting a college access and success agenda with priorities in the regional business sector means SoCal CAN needs to have a presence in new forums not typically inhabited by social sector organizations, such as chambers of commerce.

- Different members have varying practices and systems for collecting data on the students they serve. This results in a data consistency challenge when the network wants to aggregate data and use it to shine light on the collective impact of network members.

- Members possess a range of relationships with people in positions of influence, such as elected officials and civic leaders. Members recognize the value of these relationships and are challenged to discover the best ways to both map them and place them in service to a unified program, communications and policy agenda.

The Network Solution

- The small but effective network management team creates opportunities to connect in-person and electronically. Meetings and virtual conversations provide a space for formal and informal sharing and for discussing strategies to improve policies and practices. For example, ten network members interested in "college retention" have formed a work group on how to support students once they enter college to help them stay enrolled. As a result, they have developed the College Retention Excels With Students (CREWS) program. This program is now seen as a model worthy of replication by a regional college access and success network in Northern California, as well as other colleague organizations across the country.

- Network management works with members to navigate sensitive issues both publicly and in quiet side discussions, helping them to consistently find common ground on which they can move ahead. SoCal CAN's unified voice has allowed them to quickly become a go-to resource in higher education advocacy circles.

- Network management has found that members prefer to address the data challenge not by having new data collection systems imposed, but by working within the systems they already have in place. SoCal CAN has worked with a statewide funder (which has granting relationships with many of the network members) to supply resources and guidance to inform an efficient data collection process and a more consistent database.

- In an effort to engage with business executives – and to strengthen connections with elected and school district officials – SoCal CAN members have pursued and received foundation funding to support efforts to cultivate these relationships.

The Successes

- SoCal CAN has helped to build a strong college access field in Southern California. Prior to the formation of the network, member organizations operated independently, with limited budgets and smaller scopes of work. Collectively, SoCal CAN is maximizing resources and broadening opportunities for the students served by each organization. In addition, the network is serving to link the funding community, academia, policy makers, school leadership, faith-based institutions and other large youth-serving organizations to the college access agenda.

- As a result of local impact and success, SoCal CAN has received national visibility. They have won significant grant funding from national funders and are participants in the Lumina Foundation for Education's national, multi-year KnowHow2Go (KH2GO) network-building initiative. KH2GO has helped SoCal CAN strengthen relationships with numerous college access and success networks in other states and has helped all the participants build and frame a common conceptual language that did not previously exist.

- SoCal CAN has successfully served as a conduit for placing high quality messages about college access in mainstream and ethnic media outlets. This has made the group a primary "go-to" resource when print and broadcast media pursue education stories.

- SoCal CAN will host a first-ever regional summit on college access and success, a symbol of the network's significance and effectiveness as a field-building asset.

- The network has influenced institutional change on college campuses. For example, SoCal CAN has helped colleges to more clearly communicate with students about how to secure college financial aid. SoCal CAN now formally advises a state university on financial aid policies and practices.

- To enhance the sustainability of the network's core functions, SoCal CAN's leadership has begun exploring ways to partner with colleges and universities that value the preparation programs the network members offer. These partnerships will serve to support the successful identification, recruitment and retention of students from low-income communities.

- The network has served as a training ground for leaders of member organizations in how to engage in policy advocacy efforts. Members have successfully executed legislative advocacy visits to elected officials and have grown adept at carrying consistent messages to elected officials about the importance of nurturing a college-going culture in their respective districts.

- SoCal CAN currently provides regular advice and guidance to other groups around the United States on how to replicate their network model.

For More Information

Go to *www.socalcollegeaccess.org*.

To access a more in-depth version of this and other related case studies, please visit *www.CommunityPartners.org/networks*.

North American Alliance for Fair Employment

Cooperating Network Example

The Issue

A wide spectrum of advocacy and activist groups, beginning in 1997, looked for a way to join together to examine the issues and promote the rights of contingent workers. Encouraged by a progressive private foundation, the groups convened a large general assembly and agreed on a network structure.

The groups wanted the network to provide a flow of useful information about contingent work issues, shape both local and national discourse on contingent work, link organizations across divides of geography, structure, program and constituency, and establish groundwork for future funder support of their activities and advocacy. But was it too much to ask?

The Challenges

In the beginning, bridging so many diverse interests seemed the most challenging: Construction workers and other labor unions, professionals from the high-tech industry, university graduate assistants and undocumented immigrants all held their own, unique perspectives and definitions regarding the same issue. But more significant hurdles would beset the membership and the network itself a few years down the road.

The Network Solution

An 18-month planning process led to the establishment of the North American Alliance for Fair Employment (NAAFE), with the purpose of garnering collective responses from otherwise fragmented groups around the broad issue of contingent work and economic restructuring.

By 2006, NAAFE consisted of 65 organizations from both Canada and the U.S. A volunteer coordinating committee received support from a small "secretariat" staffed by three people. Action groups addressed specific priorities such as the development and advocacy of a "temporary workers' bill of rights," to the operators of agencies placing temporary workers in business settings. Member organizations can point to a number of important accomplishments achieved by the network, not the least of which was an annual (and, later, biannual) general assembly at which members shared with one another both successes and challenges encountered in their individual organizations.

With significantly diminished foundation grant funding prospects, and no provision in place for member groups to self-finance the network, NAAFE's initial high energy dissipated. NAAFE merged under another organization, Massachusetts Global Action (MGA), and MGA staff refocused NAAFE activities sharply. Two critical issues propelled the realignment: (1) a lack of clarity regarding the authority of staff versus the coordinating committee, a problem with roots in the original network agreement, and (2) the perceived, potential or actual influence of private funders as well as belief on the part of members that funder affiliation might lead to greater individual member grants.

The Successes

Despite its challenges, NAAFE achieved not just longevity, but a number of concrete and very positive results, including:

- Coordination that led to greater focus in New England on rising anti-immigrant movement issues.
- Development of a delegation of 50 people who attended the World Social Forum/Caucus on issues in globalization in January 2006.
- Several key publications widely disseminated in the field.
- Creation of a useful and easily accessible website as a resource for members and other groups.

For More Information

Go to *www.fairjobs.org* or *www.massglobalaction.org.*

To access a more in-depth version of this and other related case studies, please visit *www.CommunityPartners.org/networks.*

The Child Care Alliance of Los Angeles

Coordinating Network Example

The Issue

The Child Care Alliance of Los Angeles, formed in 1997, is a network of 13 public and private agencies working together to coordinate the delivery of early education and childcare services throughout Los Angeles County. The agencies provide a variety of services, which include responding to parents and families seeking information on available child care facilities and providers. Alliance agencies also provide childcare subsidies in the form of vouchers to qualified low-income families. Serving over 55,000 children annually, the agencies collectively touch the lives of every child in Los Angeles County assisted with public childcare subsidy funds. In total, the member agencies manage close to $500 million a year in childcare subsidy dollars provided through federal agencies and the State of California and channeled through the County of Los Angeles.

The Challenges

Initial challenges in creating this network involved forging sufficient cohesion and a sense of equal partnership among child care groups of greatly varying size and scope. Member organization leaders were challenged to build a unified voice in the public policy arena and align the content of individual organizations' government agency contracts.

The majority of representatives to the network are CEO's, which brings agency decision makers directly to the network table. Because client populations and capacities among the member groups continually change and evolve, a network management challenge has been to facilitate effective decision making and to resolve equity issues that arise among such a forceful and powerful group of agency executives.

California has faced extensive turmoil in recent years, challenging network members and management to respond rapidly, strategically and effectively to government program priorities and to shifting dynamics in the policy environment. Network members strive to reach consensus on issues, but the nature of the government contracts they have in common naturally affects every member agency's operations, focus and priorities in differing ways. The network management succeeds in focusing on immediate matters related to contract coordination and mediation among network members. However, an opportunity still unrealized in the network is to find sufficient common ground – and the investment of executive leadership time – to focus new strategies and initiatives that would help diversify and expand the collective and individual work of member agencies.

Finally, any turmoil with public sector budgets – and California has faced extensive turmoil in recent years

– challenges network members and management to respond rapidly, strategically and effectively to government program priorities and to the shifting dynamics of an often-conflicted policy environment. Network members strive to reach consensus on issues, but the nature of the government contracts they have in common naturally affects every member agency's operations, focus and priorities in differing ways. The network management succeeds in focusing on immediate matters related to contract coordination and mediation among network members. An opportunity still unrealized in the network is to find sufficient common ground – and the investment of time of busy leaders – to focus new strategies and initiatives that would help diversify and expand the collective and individual work of member agencies.

The Network Solution

Diversifying and expanding the range of funding sources available for the network's core operations occupies the current focus of member discussion, exploration and action. Network members have considered continuing the self-assessment scheme currently in place – which determines contributions based on the size and scope of various public contracts the network negotiates for members – but they have also considered ways to diminish their current dependence on a funding scheme tied to government contracts. For example, they have considered augmenting network core support with grants from private foundations for special-focus projects.

Members realize that the network needs to help all of its

members adopt a more flexible and adaptive approach to the network purpose which, until now, has concentrated almost exclusively on aligning network member contracts and other internal capacities with the requirements of government funding. Member meetings need to move from focusing on contracts to creating space, time and incentives for joint planning of field-advancing projects and programs. Network members have the potential to position themselves as thought leaders, developing and promoting creative solutions to helping children in low-income families move to higher levels of economic, social and educational prosperity. Members have begun to understand how valuable such a move would be for the 13 member agencies, especially at a time when the program and public policy landscape is in flux.

The Successes

The overall success of the network includes:

- Commitment by member agencies to fund their collective work together using a variety of funding sources. New projects and programs are negotiated collectively with an understanding that a portion of grants or contracts is needed to fund the small network staff and infrastructure.
- A groundbreaking model involving a countywide approach to unprecedented levels of early education and childcare service coordination.
- A public policy and advocacy platform that targets local, state and federal government agencies concerned with child development and care.

- Effective negotiation on behalf of 13 agencies to win joint contracts with government agencies and prominent decision makers.

For More Information

Go to *www.ccala.net*

To access a more in-depth version
of this and other related case studies, please visit
www.CommunityPartners.org/networks.

The California Partnership

Coordinating Network Example

The Issue

After working together on an effort to influence federal policy around jobs and income for poor families, a diverse group of community-based advocacy and service organizations from Los Angeles sought to harness their collective power with a statewide coalition of their own. But how to connect such a large, disparate group?

The Challenges

Initial challenges to creating a network were many. Groups were distinct and disconnected in their work, their advocacy efforts often overlapped and their messages to legislators were uncoordinated. Spread far and wide across the state, they tended to identify their constituencies quite differently. Even with the network in place, members still occasionally lost sight of their common ties with one another and conflicts arose.

The Network Solution

A responsive, representative structure, a clearly defined and realistic set of mutual expectations, and fiscal support:

success by the California Partnership on these critical fronts has helped unite dozens of groups as an effective coordinating network in the fight against poverty in California.

Each of the network's five chapters sends one or more representatives to the nine-member Coordinating Committee. The Coordinating Committee's job is to strike the right balance between network priorities and member organization missions. The committee supports member engagement by hearing and shaping various views. Committee representatives then set priorities based on member input, keeping the network's unifying purpose at the forefront. This principle – shared purpose goes first – has helped surface and resolve conflicts when friction over priorities arose between some members of the network.

All member organizations sign the network memo of understanding, an agreement outlining member responsibilities to the network. The Center for Community Change serves as the group's fiscal sponsor but does not direct the network.

The Successes

Overall, network members experience a sense of collective strength and accomplish more as a network. Concrete results they point to are:

- Greater civic engagement in target communities through the publication and wide distribution of a Voter Guide in six languages.

- A successful tax fairness campaign that included extensive educational activities, outreach, and a tool kit written in English, Spanish and Chinese.
- Legislative testimony and mass mobilization in opposition to proposals in the 2006 California budget process that would have hurt low-income families.
- Unified co-sponsorship and advocacy for SB1639, the "Education Works" bill, which the Governor signed into law.

For More Information

Go to *www.california-partnership.org* where you can find a copy of the agreement executed by The California Partnership's participating members.

To access a more in-depth version of this and other related case studies, please visit *www.CommunityPartners.org/networks.*

The Water Forum

Collaborating Network Example

The Issue

Water was and remains the hot-button issue for the Sacramento region of California. By the early 1990s, efforts to manage the water supply while preserving the area's ecological habitat had developed into a contentious, litigious mess. Developers, water purveyors, environmentalists, business owners and executives, agricultural leaders and representatives of various citizen groups all wanted to have a say. But how could so many diverse stakeholders bridge those various interests and objectives with the goal of one workable solution?

The Challenges

The issue alone required a solution on a grand scale. One that would not only involve multiple stakeholders and differing interests and agendas, but that would be an ongoing process for decades to come. With long-standing conflicts added to the mix, the issue could have seemed insurmountable. It wasn't just environmentalists suing the water interests, but the water suppliers suing each other. The City and County of Sacramento in

1995 convened the Water Forum in an effort to bring the diverse groups involved closer to a shared way of approaching the problem. They had a long road ahead in addressing the historical feelings of distrust and ill will resulting from highly adversarial relationships.

The Network Solution

The Water Forum in 2001 became a formalized network, with 40 members signing a historic agreement to work together with common purpose through the year 2030. But this unifying act did not come without years of patience, commitment on the part of all parties involved, significant financial support and, most essential by all accounts, a mediation process ideally suited to the challenges at hand.

All members underwent a common education process led by Susan Sherry, Ph.D. prior to entering into a type of mediation called "interest- based negotiation," which focuses on assuring that all voices are heard equally and fairly. Lawsuits were dropped, and the diverse group of stakeholders developed an understanding of one another's concerns and the ability to work together toward a common goal.

A dedicated professional staff provides basic management and a 16-member coordinating committee makes policy decisions around dues, budgets and oversight of major work projects. Flexibility, constant communication, inarguable success and a general "pride of ownership" keep the network moving forward productively.

The Successes

The time and commitment members have invested in the Water Forum have paid off for the region. Some of their results include:

- Improved water flow.
- Conservation efforts.
- Expanded groundwater management.
- Habitat programs.
- New water treatment plants.
- Diversion of the American River.
- Replicated networks in other counties.
- Exceptional personal and professional relationships among leaders in the water community.

For More Information

Go to *www.waterforum.org* where you can find a copy of the agreement executed by the Water Forum's participating members.

To access a more in-depth version of this and other related case studies, please visit *www.CommunityPartners.org/networks*.

Position Description

Sample Job Description for a Network Manager

Position Title:
Network Manager (alternatively: Network Coordinator, Network Facilitator)

Accountable To:
Network Membership through [Network Coordinating Group, or other reporting channel]

Summary of Organizational Role:
The Network Manager serves as a key coordinative and facilitative resource to members of the network. The Network Manager helps the network members reach and fulfill the network purpose based on agreements negotiated by members and expressed in the network agreement.

Compensation:
[$ amount or "commensurate with experience"]

Duties and Responsibilities:

- Facilitate network member communication, information sharing, interest clarification, and identification and resolution of differences.

- Support directly – or identify and coordinate with outside resources that can support – members with interest negotiation, conflict resolution, meeting management and other needed skills.
- Work with members to identify, clarify and periodically revisit network purpose. Facilitate member development and periodically evaluate and realign network priorities, tasks and activities in ways that advance network effectiveness and shared network member results.
- Guide, smooth and support efficient interactions among members engaged in network's tasks.
- Counsel network members on how to align work and results in the network setting with strategic planning and program work inside their own organizations to achieve greater synchronicity between the two settings.
- Facilitate data collection necessary for assessing and evaluating effectiveness of network activities.
- Identify favorable opportunities members can pursue that address and resolve issues critical to network success.
- Locate, help secure and budget financial and other resources needed to support network operations.
- Build the network by supporting members in identification and recruitment of new members and helping to orient and integrate new members to the network's history, agreements, decisions, challenges and requirements.
- Facilitate ways to refresh and renew network capabilities, function and focus.

Position Requirements:

- Demonstrated knowledge of and established reputation in the field of [name field or area of interest of the network].
- Demonstrated ability to work productively and masterfully in complex, inter-organizational settings among groups with differing interests.
- Conflict identification, negotiation and resolution skills and experience.
- Outstanding oral and written communications skills.
- Flexibility, adaptability and integrity.

Network Agreement

Sample Template for a Network Agreement

No network agreement resembles any other agreement. All have unique features particular to the network and its members. Virtually all are voluntary in nature and members decide and enforce explicit standards of accountability. Still, groups developing network agreements, charters, relational contracts or memoranda of understanding should address some or all of the following points in the final written product, depending on the type of network they are developing:

Reasons for Agreement:

- Describes background rationale for forming the network (perhaps in preamble form).
- Outlines expected duration of the agreement (if intent is to operate for a specific period, otherwise specifies "open-ended" timeframe).

Network Purpose

- Describes the specific shared purpose binding members in common cause.

- Outlines any subsidiary aims that flow from the purpose.

Network Priorities

This section includes initial agreements about critical and urgent priorities network members will address. Because priorities change, this summary of agreed-upon priorities must anticipate flexibility and change – sometimes on short notice – and include provisions for periodic updating. Members must expect that priorities will develop and change as the network develops and changes. Changes in the external environment, such as in societal conditions, government priorities and member organization leadership shifts, may affect the work of the network. Initial priorities may be listed here and amended by agreement of the network governing body and membership for inclusion in an addendum or another form of communication that all members participate in affirming.

Membership

Includes:

- List of establishing members who are signers of the current agreement.
- Membership qualifications for organizations and institutions.
- Requirements and process for admitting new members and how they will be oriented.

- Any special forms or categories of membership and the requirements for maintaining such status (observer, individual expert, advisor, etc.).
- Provisions, reasons, sanctions, processes and procedures for removing members if necessary.

Roles and Commitments of Members

Describes collective member responsibility and expectations, including:

- Commitment to the shared purpose.
- Willingness to participate in setting network priorities and accomplishing the tasks and activities agreed to by all.
- Commitment to shared "ownership" of the network and its accomplishments.
- Acknowledgment of potential risks and rewards that accompany participation.
- Commitment to open communication, civility and equal partnership.
- Member commitment to joint decision making processes.
- Specific monetary and other resources members must commit and contribute.
- General types of activities/tasks expected of members (for meetings, action group participation, etc.).
- Duration of time commitment expected of members to network participation (commitment can be open-ended or – depending on the type of network – it may be desirable to specify a year or more).
- Describes specific authority of a member organization's representative to make decisions on

behalf of his/her organization and devote time and commit organizational resources to accomplishing network tasks and activities.
- Describes procedure network will follow if/when member organizations change their representative to the network.

Operational Structure and Procedures

Describes:

- Network governance structure, including composition of oversight or administrative coordination committee and approach to how meetings will be chaired, facilitated or conducted.
- Procedures for developing and periodically reviewing the shared purpose and network priorities.
- System by which members will voluntarily hold themselves accountable for accepting and engaging in work toward agreed-upon priorities.
- Procedure for constituting work or action groups.
- Procedure to assess and deal with changed internal and external conditions that may affect the work of the network.
- Procedure for tackling and resolving (not avoiding) conflict.
- Procedure for reaching consensus, negotiating, voting, or other processes for moving from deliberation through decisions and into tasks and activities.
- Procedures for deciding on and implementing member training (such as in negotiation, meeting management, decision making, listening skills, relationship building techniques).

- Procedure for members to consider and integrate network priorities and work results into their own organizational and institutional strategic planning.

Role of Staff and Other Needed Support

Describes:

- Network manager job description.
- Conditions for tapping and using consultants, experts and other outside resources. (This depends on the type of network, some of which will not have staff.)

Funding and Resources

- Reiterates and summarizes each member's specific expected financial, time and resource contributions, including arrangements for "self-taxing" when applicable.
- May contain agreements with or references to separate agreements for resource commitments from key stakeholders.
- Describes process for acquiring resources for network, including how network members will approach funders.
- Describes budget for network, if budgeted expenses are anticipated.

Accountability

Describes:

- Member commitment to accountability, to engaging in periodic assessment and evaluation, valuing feedback, etc.
- Frequency of review and evaluation.
- Process for conducting periodic review and evaluation of network effectiveness, accomplishments, structure, functionality, etc. including analysis of internal network operation and process for gathering external perceptions from various stakeholders, including but not limited to network members.
- Actions network will take as a result of the evaluations.

Useful Resources and Websites

Agranoff, R. (2003). *Leveraging networks: A guide for public managers working across organizations.* Arlington, VA: IBM Endowment for The Business of Government.

Agranoff, R. (2007). *Managing networks: Adding value to public organizations.* Washington, DC: Georgetown University Press.

Agranoff, R., & McGuire, M. (2003). *Collaborative public management: New strategies for local governments.* Washington, DC: Georgetown University Press.

Anklam, P. (2007). *Net work: A practical guide to creating and sustaining networks at work and in the world.* Burlington, MA: Elsevier.

The Annie E. Casey Foundation. (1993). *The path of most resistance.* Baltimore, MD: The Annie E. Casey Foundation.

Bardach, E. (1998). *Getting agencies to work together: The practice and theory of managerial craftsmanship.* Washington, DC: Brookings Institute Press.

Bradach, J. (2010). Scaling impact. *Stanford Social Innovation Review, Summer,* 27-28.

Briggs, X. d. S. (2001, June). Networks, power, and a dual agenda: New lessons and strategies for old community building dilemmas. In *Working smarter in community development, knowledge in action brief.* Retrieved from http://web.mit.edu/1workingsmarter/allreadings/

Brown, K. A., & Keast, R. L. (2003) Citizen-government engagement: Community connection through networked arrangements. *Asian Journal of Public Administration,* 25(1), 107-131.

Connick, S. (2006). The Sacramento area water forum: A case study. *IURD Working Paper Series, Institute of Urban & Regional Development.* Berkeley, CA: University of California, Berkley. Retrieved from http://escholarship.org/uc/item/8fn9d21c?display=all

Cordero-Guzmán, Héctor R. (2004.) Interorganizational networks among community-based organizations. In E. Meléndez, (Ed.), *Communities and Workforce Development* (pp. 411-438). Kalamazoo, MI: W. E. Upjohn Institute for Employment Research.

Crowley, C. M. (2004). Joined up governance: Pushing the youth policy boundaries? *Public Administration Today, 2* (Dec-Feb), 46-53.

Doyle, M., & Straus, D. (1993). *How to Make Meetings Work.* New York, NY: Penguin Group.

Edwards, S. L., Stern, R. F., & Cornerstone Consulting Group, Inc. (1998). Building and sustaining community partnerships for teen pregnancy prevention. [A working paper]. Retrieved from http://aspe.hhs.gov/hsp/teenp/teenpreg/teenpreg.htm

Goldsmith, S., & Eggers, W. D. (2004). *Governing by network: The new shape of the public sector.* Washington, DC: Brookings Institution Press.

Goldsmith, S., Georges, G., & Burke, T. G. (2010). *The power of social innovation: How civic entrepreneurs ignite community networks for good.* San Francisco, CA: Jossey Bass.

Gray, B. (1989). *Collaborating: Finding common ground for multiparty problems.* San Francisco, CA: Jossey-Bass.

Hanf, K., & Sharpf, F. W. (Eds.). (1979). *Interorganizational policy making: Limits to coordination and central control.* London, England: Sage Publications.

Himmelman, A. T. (2001). On coalitions and transformation of power relations: Collaborative betterment and collaborative empowerment. *American Journal of Community Psychology, 29*(2), 277-284.

Huxham, C. (Ed.). (1996). *Creating collaborative advantage.* London, England: Sage Publications.

Huxham, C., & Vangen S. (2005). *Managing to collaborate: The theory and practice of collaborative advantage.* London, England: Routledge.

Innes, J. E., & Booher, D. E. (1999). Consensus building as role playing and bricolage. *Journal of the American Planning Association, 65*(1), 9-26.

Innes, J. E., & Booher, D. E. (2010). *Planning with complexity: An introduction to collaborative Rationality for Public Policy.* London, England: Routledge.

Kamensky, J. M., & Burlin, T. J. (Eds.). (2004). *Collaboration: Using networks and partnerships.* Lanham, MD: Rowman & Littlefield Publishers, Inc.

Kania, J., & Kramer, M. (2011). Collective impact. *Stanford Social Innovation Review, Winter,* 36-41.

Kearns, M. Netcentric advocacy: Advocacy for the age of connectivity. [Web log]. http://www.network-centricadvocacy.net/

Keast, R. (2011). Joined-up governance in Australia: How the past can inform the future. *International Journal of Public Administration, 34*(4), 221-231.

Keast, R., Brown, K., & Mandell, M. (2007). Getting the right mix: Unpacking meanings and strategies. *International Public Management Journal, 10*(1), 9-33.

Keast, R., Mandell, M. P., Brown, K., & Woolcock, G.. (2004). Network structures: Working differently and changing expectations. *Public Administration Review, 64*(3), 363-371.

Kickert, W. J. M., Klijn, E.-H., & Koppenjan, J. F. M. (1997). *Managing complex networks: Strategies for the public sector.* London, England: Sage Publications.

Koppenjan, J., & Klijn, E-H. (2004). *Managing uncertainties in networks.* London, England: Routledge.

Lipnack, J., & Stamps, J. (1994). *The age of the network: Organizing principles for the 21st century.* Essex Junction, VT: Oliver Wight Publications.

Mandell, M. P. (1999). The impact of collaborative efforts: Changing the face of public policy through networks and network structures. *Review of Policy Research, 16*(1), 4-17.

Mandell, M. P. (2000). A revised look at management in network structures. *International Journal of Organization Theory and Behavior, 3*(1-2), 185-210.

Mandell, M. P. (2001). Collaboration through network structures for community building efforts. *National Civic Review, 90*(3) 279-288.

Mandell, M. P (Ed.). (2001). *Getting results through collaboration: networks and network structures for public policy and management.* Westport, CT: Quorum Books.

Mandell, M. P. (2002). Different types of collaborations and why the difference really matters. *The Public Manager, 31*(4), 36-40.

Mandell, M., & Harrington, M. (1999). *When collaboration is not enough: Learning from our CITIES (Community initiatives that increase everyone's strengths).* Los Angeles, CA: The Los Angeles Roundtable For Children.

Mandell, M., & Keast, R. L. (2007). Evaluating network arrangements: Toward revised performance measures. *Public Performance & Management Review, 30*(4), 574-597.

Mandell, M., Keast, R. (2009). A new look at leadership in collaborative networks: Process catalysts. In J. Raffel, P. Lisinik, & A. Middlebrook (Eds.), *Public Sector Leadership: International Challenges and Perspectives.* (pp.163-178). Northampton, MA: Edward Elgar.

Mandell, M., & Steelman, T. (2003). Understanding what can be accomplished through interorganizational innovations: The importance of typologies, context and management strategies. *Public Management Review, 5*(2), 197-224.

McGuire, M. (2002). Managing networks: Propositions on what managers do and why they do it. *Public Management Review, 62*(5), 599-609.

Merisotis, J. P. (2010) President's message: Networks can multiply the power of change. In P. L. Brennan, Lumina *Foundation Lessons, Spring, 3*.

Miward, H. B., & Provan, K. G. (2006). *A manager's guide to choosing and using collaborative networks*. Washington, DC: IBM Center for Business of Government.

Montgomery, C. (2004). Learning together: Collaborative inquiry among grant makers and grantees. Retrieved from http://grantcraft.net/index.cfm?fuseaction=Page.ViewPage&pageId=1541

Moodliar, Foltz, Costello & Brecher. (2004). Making networks work: Preliminary observations from NAFFE's structured advocacy network. Retrieved from http://www.fairjobs.org/archive/node/7

O'Leary, R., & Blomgren Bingham , L. (Eds.). (2009). *The collaborative public manager: New ideas for the twenty-first century*. Washington, DC: Georgetown University Press.

O'Leary, R., Gerard, C, & Blomgren Bingham, L. (2006). Introduction to the symposium on collaborative public management. *Public Administration Review, 66*(Issue supplement, s1) 6-9.

O'Toole, Jr., L. J. (1997). Treating networks seriously: Practical and research-based agendas in public administration. *Public Administration Review, 57*(1), 45-52.

Plastrik, P., & Taylor, M. (2010). Network power for philanthropy and nonprofits. Boston, MA: The Pilot House. Retrieved from http://www.barrfoundation.org/news/network-power-for-philanthropy-and-nonprofits/

Public Education Network. (2010). *KnowHow2Go: Network rubric workbook.*

Remley, D. (1998). Pool resources for success. *Nonprofit World, 16*(5), 42-45.

Ring, P. S., Huxham, C., Ebers, M., & Cropper, S. (Eds.). (2008). *The Oxford handbook of inter-organizational relations.* Oxford: Oxford University Press.

Scearce, D. *Catalyzing networks for social change: A funder's guide.* Washington, DC: Grantmakers for Effective Organizations. Retrieved from http://www.geofunders.org/home.aspx

Steffen, A. (2007). The future of philanthropy: Innovation, networks, thought leaders and the fringe. Retrieved from http://www.worldchanging.com/archives/006796.html

Traynor, B. (2009). Vertigo and the intentional inhabitant: Leadership in a connected world. Retrieved from http://www.nonprofitquarterly.org/index.php?option=com_content&view=article&id=1384:vertigo-and-the-intentional-inhabitant-leadership-in-a-connected-world&catid=154:current-issue

Wei-Skillern, J., & Marciano, S. (2008). The networked nonprofit. *Stanford Social Innovation Review, Spring,* 38-43.

Yang, K., & Bergrud, E. (Eds.). (2008). *Civic engagement in a network society.* Charlotte, N.C.: Information Age Publishing, Inc.